Praise for *1947*

"Even though I have a history degree and already knew at least a little about many of the events Åsbrink details, I found so much that was eye-opening in every month's account."

—Nancy Pearl, NPR, Best Books of the Year

"Evocative…Åsbrink is throughout attentive to the complex dynamic produced by the Holocaust's multiple aftermaths, the urgently necessary and terrifyingly confusing process of decolonization and the consolidation of the Soviet bloc…Ultimately most compelling is 1947's relationship to our present.

—*New York Times Book Review*

"1947 is a particularly alluring inflection point…The conviction that the past is never really past, that it is always striking back, animates Åsbrink's work…she creates a sense of history unfolding in real time."

—*New Republic*

"A skillful and illuminating way of presenting, to wonderful effect, the cultural, political and personal history of a year that changed the world."

—*Kirkus Reviews*

"This superb book deserves a wide audience. In telling history through disparate voices, Åsbrink effectively describes the seas of change, as times change quicker than people do."

—*Library Journal* (starred review)

"[Åsbrink's] story develops a power that needs no metaphor to help explain it. It's a tale of the things that make up the essence of human existence: love, family, uncertainty, horror, belonging."

—*Star Tribune*

"[A] remarkable work of reportage…a compelling collage of events."

—*Literary Hub*

"Unearthing many forgotten details, Åsbrink illuminates this pivotal year after the end of WWII, adroitly revealing how profoundly 1947 shaped the decades that followed... Åsbrink writes with sardonic passion in an immediately striking tone... A sweeping cacophony of modernity."
—*Booklist*

"Informative, provocative and also very personal." —*Boston Herald*

"A fascinating, horrifying and illuminating portrayal of circumstances that have impacted the present day." —*Shelf Awareness*

"Åsbrink writes sentences that make one gasp in admiration... [*1947*] should be read for its poetry, its insights, and the interweaving of personal and political judgments." —*Sydney Morning Herald*

"Extraordinarily inventive and gripping, a uniquely personal account of a single, momentous year."
—Philippe Sands, author of *East West Street*

"This is history as a series of eclectic snapshots of events and episodes and people, from the Nuremberg Trials to the partition of India, during a year in which the world tried to redefine its hopes and come to terms with its failures: and it makes for fascinating, disquieting, lively and often surprising reading."
—Caroline Moorehead, author of *Village of Secrets*

"Lucid and vivid... An outstanding work, history as it should be told."
—Salil Tripathi, Chair of the PEN International Writers in Prison Committee, and author of *The Colonel Who Would Not Repent*

"Åsbrink deftly brings together the tangle, the mess, the aspirations and the disappointments which characterized the period and which for her resonate personally through her family history."
—Rosemary Ashton, author of *One Hot Summer: Dickens, Darwin, Disraeli, and the Great Stink of 1858*

1947

WHERE NOW BEGINS

ELISABETH ÅSBRINK

translated from the Swedish by
FIONA GRAHAM

Other Press
New York

First softcover printing 2019
ISBN 978-1-63542-012-8

Originally published in Swedish as *1947* by Natur & Kultur, Stockholm, in 2016

First published in English by Scribe, London, in 2017

Production editor: Yvonne E. Cárdenas

This book was set in Stempel Garamond.

10 9 8 7 6 5 4 3 2 1

Printed in the United States of America on acid-free paper. For information write to Other Press LLC, 267 Fifth Avenue, 6th Floor, New York, NY 10016. Or visit our Web site: www.otherpress.com

LIBRARY OF CONGRESS CATALOGING-IN-PUBLICATION DATA

Names: Åsbrink, Elisabeth, author. | Graham, Fiona, (translator of Swedish), translator.
Title: 1947 : where now begins / Elisabeth Åsbrink ; translated from the Swedish by Fiona Graham.
Other titles: 1947, where now begins | Nineteen forty-seven, where now begins
Description: New York : Other Press, [2018]
Identifiers: LCCN 2017040450 (print) | LCCN 2017054651 (ebook) | ISBN 9781590518960 (hardcover) | ISBN 9781590518977 (ebook)
Subjects: LCSH: Nineteen forty-seven, A.D. | Civilization, Modern—20th century. | History, Modern—20th century—Chronology. | Holocaust, Jewish (1939–1945)—Influence.
Classification: LCC CB425 (print) | LCC CB425 .A768 (ebook) | DDC 909.82—dc23 LC record available at https://lccn.loc.gov/2017044651

In den Flüssen nördlich der Zukunft
werf ich das Netz aus, das du
zögernd beschwerst
mit von Steinen geschriebenen
Schatten.

In the rivers north of the future
I cast the net you
haltingly weight
with stone-written
shadows.

— Paul Celan
Translation after John Felstiner

The time is not quite what it ought to be.

On January 1, 1947, *The Times* informs the people of Great Britain that they cannot rely on their clocks. To be quite certain that the time is what it purports to be, they are to tune in to the BBC, which will broadcast extra bulletins in order to keep track of it.

Electric clocks are affected by the frequent power cuts. Mechanical ones also need overhauling. Maybe it's the cold. Maybe things will improve.

The war has seen nearly 50,000 tons of bombs dropped on London by the Luftwaffe. More than 4.5 million buildings in Britain are damaged. Some towns have been all but wiped out, such as the Scottish port whose airraids even got a name of their own: the Clydebank Blitz.

All across Europe, there is damage. The Austrian city Wiener Neustadt once had 4,000 buildings; now only 18 are intact. A third of the houses in Budapest are uninhabitable. In France, 460,000 buildings are in ruins. In the Soviet Union, 1,700 small towns and villages have been demolished. In Germany, around 3.6 million apartments have been blitzed — a fifth of the country's homes. Half the homes in Berlin itself are derelict. In Germany as a whole, over 18 million people are homeless. A further 10 million in Ukraine have no roof over their heads. All of them have to cope with having only limited access to water and a sporadic electricity supply.

Human rights are nonexistent, and hardly anyone has heard of the crime of genocide. Those who survived have only just begun to count their dead. Many travel home, without finding it; others travel anywhere except back where they come from.

Europe's countryside has been razed and plundered, and tracts of land are flooded by sabotaged dams. Fields, woodland, farmsteads — lives, food, livelihoods — lie under ash, covered in sludge.

Greece lost a third of its forests during the German occupation. Over a thousand villages there have been burned to the ground. In Yugoslavia, over half the country's livestock have been slaughtered, and the plundering of grain, milk, and wool has left the economy in ruins. Not only did Hitler's and Stalin's armies wreak destruction as they advanced, but they were ordered to destroy everything in their path when they retreated. This scorched-earth tactic was intended to leave nothing behind for the enemy's troops. In the words of Heinrich Himmler: "Not one person, no cattle, no quintal of grain, no railway track must remain behind ... The enemy must find a country totally burned and destroyed."

Now, after the war, everyone is on the lookout for watches — stealing, hiding, mislaying, or losing them. The time remains indeterminate. When it's eight in the evening in Berlin, it's seven in Dresden, but nine in Bremen. Russian time prevails in the Russian zone, while the British impose summer time on their part of Germany. If someone asks what time the clock says, most will say it's gone. The clock, that is — or do they mean time itself?

JANUARY

'Arab al-Zubayd

Hamdeh Jom'a is a strong-willed girl, but somewhere there is a limit. And it is getting closer.

When the man with the magic box comes to the village, he calls the children together. The little ones are to ask their mothers for grain, the older ones are to pilfer food, but everyone has to come to see the magic box, which — so the man claims — eats sugar and shits sweets. They laugh and pay him in bulgur wheat, lentils, and oats. He tells his tales and shows his pictures, which turn into stories when he puts a stick into the cardboard box and stirs.

Hamdeh is sixteen and can't get enough of the moving pictures' magic. She filches bread from her mother to pay the man, takes handfuls of lentils from the stores. She thinks of her uncle, who owns a great many hens and five cockerels. During his afternoon nap, she sneaks in and steals some eggs — just so she can see the pictures moving again, hear about heroes and freedom fighters, feel the world expand. But as she leaves her uncle's tent with the eggs, he awakes, catches the girl, and strikes her. The eggs are smashed, and that night Hamdeh, her apron soiled, sleeps in a cave to avoid his anger. But that blows over.

Every evening, when he has told his stories to an end, the

man with the magic box concludes with the same words: "This is the darkness, this is the night."

Washington

In the Oval Office at the White House, President Truman sits writing his diary. He wakes early on January 6 and fits in a few hours' work before strolling down to the station to meet his family. A good 35-minute walk, he notes, glad to have his wife and daughter back home. The great white jail is a hellish place to be alone. The floors creak and crack at night. It takes little imagination for him to picture old James Buchanan wandering back and forth, full of anxiety over a world beyond his control. In fact, the unquiet spirits of many presidents traipse up and down the stairs, complaining about what they should have done better and what they failed to achieve. Some of his late predecessors are absent, Truman writes in the blue diary. They simply don't have the time, being far too busy controlling heaven and governing hell. But the others, the poor, tormented presidents who were misrepresented in history, get no rest. The White House is a hellish place.

London

It is announced on January 7 that 500 women employed by London Transport have to vacate their posts. They're being sent home. In the months to come, all London's bus and tram conductresses will be dismissed — 10,000 of them altogether. The men are back.

Malmö

Movements at the border, trees like black lines in a white landscape; footsteps on frozen ground leave few traces. The world is full of fugitives eager to escape. Some borders are less tightly controlled than others, the roads narrow and winding, the locals occupied with their own affairs.

A border between Germany and Denmark; another between Denmark and Sweden; maritime boundaries; land borders; lines drawn on paper maps, but in reality marked by a stone, a fence, a thousand dry stalks of grass rustling in the passing wind.

Many are fleeing from their experiences, others from the consequences of their acts. Silence. Secrecy. Coded messages, and never more than one night in the same place. Men stream out of Germany into Denmark and continue their journey toward Sweden. Helping hands provide them with food and a bed for the night along the way.

Per Engdahl wants his passport back. Denied it, he finds himself confined to his own country, which he wants both to preserve and to expand until the borders give way. This is a contradictory vision which he will work tirelessly to realize. The Swedish Security Service classes him as a Nazi, and after a visit to Vidkun Quisling in wartime Norway, and a subsequent journey to Finland on which he met some of the Wehrmacht's top brass, his passport has been confiscated. Although Engdahl makes several attempts to recover it, this takes a while — so he has others come to him, to Malmö. He has loyal collaborators who travel and organize things on his behalf. Barely any documents remain, and only a few names are mentioned in the papers that survive him.

Only through detours, unraveling threads of facts, seeking out and piecing together the events of the months that form 1947, can information be found about a time when everything seemed possible, as it had already happened.

They come from all corners of Europe. Most have fought in SS divisions on the Eastern Front, and many Balts are at risk of extradition to the Soviet Union. All of them need help to evade the consequences of their wartime actions, and the man without a passport welcomes them.

Though Per Engdahl is the leader of Sweden's Fascists, he wants to keep the white flow of fugitives seeking his aid outside the movement, discreetly concealed and coded. Thus his own home — 2, Mäster Henriksgatan, Malmö — becomes the center of operations. The fugitives' reception takes on a literary character; the Fascist, who also writes poetry, uses book titles as code words for "refugee," "hiding place," and "movement" — all to keep the Swedish police unaware.

How many come? No one is sure. Who are they? No one knows. However, among the thousands of men on the run, one or two become more than just a name — maybe even a friend. One such is Professor Johann von Leers, the right-hand man and protégé of Propaganda Minister Goebbels, and one of the most influential ideologues behind the Nazis' hate propaganda. An iron-willed, committed Jew-hater, belonging to the Nazi leadership. Von Leers was captured by US troops and interned in Darmstadt, but fled after 18 months. After that, he left only diffuse and contradictory traces. He managed to disappear altogether for several years, making a definite reappearance in 1950, in Buenos Aires. Some claim he went underground in northern Germany for several years; others say he lived incognito in Italy.

What we do know is that in late 1946 he travels to the old merchant city of Flensburg, not far from the Danish border. He is met there by a Danish SS volunteer, Vagner Kristensen, who guides him to Padborg in Denmark, a distance of just over six miles.

"We took the refugees along a path, across a marsh, and over the border."

The young Kristensen takes a liking to Johann von Leers — they will stay in touch — and escorts his new friend further across Denmark to Copenhagen, where others take over, arranging a boat over the Öresund strait.

"They were obliged to come to me when I couldn't travel," Engdahl would later reminisce with a certain pride, though he carefully avoided letting slip a single name.

Engdahl and his friends manage to find jobs for a thousand or so Nazi fugitives. Kockums shipbuilders and Addo, the calculator manufacturer, are happy to take them on, provided that Engdahl avoids mentioning it in his magazine, *Vägen Framåt*. All of them know the score: action is fine, but in obscurity, away from the light.

Per Engdahl: poet, journalist, Fascist leader. The Swedish police regard him as the real founder of Swedish Nazism.

"Even before the war he was known as the Swedish Nazi with the best connections in international Nazism. He was *persona grata* in Berlin and Rome ... By the end of 1945, Engdahl had already contacted the remaining Nazi and Fascist cells outside Sweden," writes the central police authority, the State Police, in a summary from the early 1950s.

Rome

Just a few days before 1946 gives way to 1947, five men gather on the Viale Regina Elena in Rome: a journalist, an archaeologist, an auditor, a trade-union leader, and a man claiming to be Benito Mussolini's illegitimate son. Together, they found the Movimento Sociale Italiano, a movement based on the same ideas and ideals as Mussolini's Fascist Party had. MSI rapidly attracts numerous supporters, and large amounts of money through private donations. Only a month or so later, local sections are set up all over Italy, and the movement can begin its work of attacking democracy and countering Communism. But not just in Italy. The movement's goals include a new Europe.

Falangists in Spain, Peronists in Argentina, British Fascists under Oswald Mosley, neo-Nazis meeting illegally in Wiesbaden under the leadership of Karl-Heinz Priester. And Per Engdahl in Sweden. They lurk under the surface, making their moves when the world is looking elsewhere. Even now, they are setting up among themselves a well-organized system of couriers to circumvent passport, visa, and currency restrictions. Soon the men will come closer together, even merge. The pent-up stillness of a pendulum about to strike back.

Poland

On January 19, elections are held in Poland. But over the course of the last few weeks, half-a-million people have been accused of collaboration with the Nazis and disenfranchised by way of punishment. Over 80,000 members and supporters of the anti-Communist party Polskie Stronnictwo Ludowe [Polish People's Party] are arrested on the eve of the elections. Around a hundred of them are murdered by Poland's secret police.

As a result, the Communists win a landslide victory.

At the 1945 Yalta Conference, Stalin promised free elections in Poland — but for the multiparty system, today is the moment of death.

Al-Mahmudiyyah

The son of an Egyptian clockmaker, Hasan al-Banna, wants to turn time towards Islam. Once he was an eager learner, willful and strong-minded like his mother, and more outgoing than his father. The time of the world was adjusted in his father's workshop, where silent dials waited for hands, tiny cogwheels lay gleaming in boxes, and the sound of a mended clock was reward enough for the effort of repairing it. The ticking, distinct and regular, showed that both the object and time itself had been restored from disorder to order, from chaos to control.

Outside Hasan's father's workshop lay Egypt with its wheat fields, the men crouching under the contemptuous gaze of the British: an unfree country. And the verses of the Qur'an were lined up as tightly as the ears of wheat in the fields.

The boy, too, learned his father's craft. Being in a room full of clocks turns an hour into friend and enemy alike. Taking a clock apart, scrutinizing its inner mechanisms, and then getting time to work again transforms time into a power that can be controlled.

Paris

An aircraft carrying Simone de Beauvoir takes off for New York. There are just ten passengers and 40 seats; boarding the plane, she already feels lost. It's as if she is leaving her life in Paris behind her. Something different, something new, is going to be revealed, and it will make her a different person. The plane is in the air. It is January 25. She writes: "I am nowhere. I am somewhere else. What is time?"

New York

Now is a time without universal human rights. But has humankind missed something it didn't know existed? Have the world's religions, seeking to shield that which is human as though it were a fragment of the divine, provided adequate protection?

The world rises out of greasy human ashes. Here and now, in the United Nations' provisional secretariat in the aircraft factory at Lake Success, universal values are to be established: new thoughts, new premises for humankind, a new morality. A person's rights are not to depend on whether they are Christian or Buddhist, on whether they were born into a family with or without assets, or on their name, sex, position, country of birth, or skin color.

Entering world history, a 60-year-old woman leads the deliberations. She has just lost her driving license for careless driving. Somewhere beneath the stream of day-to-day political happenings and her sadness at the death of her husband, Franklin D. Roosevelt, somewhere beneath the layer of thoughts about aging, motherhood, and the fact that people are unused to a female leader, run the words that will follow the working party from this first day to the last, the same regardless of whether one reads the Confucian philosopher Mencius or the twelfth chapter of Paul's Letter to the Romans: "Do not be overcome by evil, but overcome evil with good."

Eleanor Roosevelt convenes her first meeting with the working party on January 27. There is a certain euphoria in the air. Never again, say the world's people to each other and themselves. Never again, say the members of the working party charged with creating human rights, who hardly grasp the magnitude of their task.

Never again. The words are repeated like the fringes on a prayer shawl, as if god existed.

Malmö

A winter wind blows through the streets of Malmö. The temporary visitor Herr von Leers excels in hatred. Once Goebbels's chief ideologue, he had proved to be an asset when it came to spreading malice.

In his pamphlet *The Jews are Looking at You*, published in 1933, he named a number of people who he believed to be Jewish — eminent German politicians, scholars, and artists — published photographs of them, and incited his fellow party members to murder them. One of them was Albert Einstein, who had already left Germany by then. "Not yet hanged," von Leers noted. But a number of the others he named were abducted and murdered, as though his words had the force of an order.

Now he is visiting Malmö.

Who purchases his ticket, who meets him at the harbor, who takes him to Per Engdahl?

He stays for a while, and the two men spend time together. What can they have discussed, what do they have in common, the Swedish Fascist leader and Goebbels's most eloquent Jew-hater? Could it be here that dreams are nurtured, that thoughts of a new future are cast in words? Is it now, in these first few days of the year, together with Johann von Leers, that Per Engdahl clarifies his vision of a postwar Europe?

The stream of SS soldiers fleeing via the Nordic countries persists. Per Engdahl sees himself as the nerve center in an organization made up of separate cells which do not know each other but are working together for a common goal: to save the courageous men in danger of punishment and extradition to hostile powers. Engdahl seems to be driven by a strong sympathy for the SS men, especially the Balts who are at risk of being deported to the Soviet Union: "We were there. We knew the score. We saw people without any really safe place anywhere in the world, people who had seen their native countries, who were being hunted like wild beasts ..."

He writes about the boats from Sweden to Spain or Latin America, but mentions in his autobiography that most SS men were sent to West Germany, regarded as relatively safe. He and his collaborators may have helped some 4,000 men, possibly slightly fewer.

A few years later, Johann von Leers will land in Buenos Aires, which boasts one of the larger colonies of Nazi criminals. President Perón is happy to receive them, not just because he sympathizes with their ideas, but also because he receives generous remuneration for his trouble from Third Reich funds. And Johann von Leers and Per Engdahl will continue to build their dreams, both separately and together.

FEBRUARY

Paris

Christian is born on February 12, or that's the way he feels. This is D-Day — as in dream, de luxe, Dior. This is the first time he is presenting a collection under his own name.

The turning points in his life are marked by fortune-tellers. Take the time when, dressed as a gypsy, he was selling lucky charms at a bazaar in his hometown of Granville. Just when it was time to pack up and go home, the hired palm-reader grasped his hand and foretold that he would make his fortune from women — a prophecy that baffled the 14-year-old boy as well as his parents. But now the reborn Christian Dior says happily: "In every country there are thin women and fat women, dark women and fair women, women of discreet taste, and others whose taste is more flamboyant. There are some women with a beautiful *décolletage*, and others whose aim is to disguise their thighs. Some are too tall. Others are too short. The world is wonderfully full of beautiful women whose shapes and tastes offer an inexhaustible diversity."

Having opened his *bureau des rêveries* just a few months previously, he selects his staff with great care. They must be focused on achieving elegance, complementing him and his dream factory with embroidery, gauze, and precision needlework. And he knows he must worship the goddess Publicity if she is to enlist Fate on his behalf.

The three-story house at 30, Avenue Montaigne, Paris, with its wrought-iron balcony and gleaming revolving door in mahogany and glass, now becomes home to his reborn persona, who lacks a past but has all the future imaginable. There, he and his colleagues labor, with feverish discipline, among folds and flounces of fabric.

Owing to the new law banning brothels throughout France, numerous women are seeking alternative employment. Christian Dior advertises for models in the press and is swamped by applications. Amid this plethora, he finds only one — Marie-Thérèse. The others — Noëlle, Paule, Yolande, Lucile, and Tania — are recruited from the world of haute couture.

They are all extremely svelte, *naturellement*, so Christian urges them to acquire false bosoms. Now is now, and everything is to be different: curves, corsets, padded hips; a waist so slender that it can be spanned by a man's hands. The New Look.

Outside, the women wear state-approved gabardine, paint their legs brown to compensate for the lack of stockings, and finish off with a darker vertical line that stands in for a seam. Their hats are large, their skirts knee-length, and their hair long, put up in a roll on their foreheads, and flowing freely down their backs as they pedal through Paris — all alike in the democracy imposed by poverty. Christian calls them Amazons, and shudders at their angular silhouettes, grainy as a wartime photograph.

For the second year in a row, the winter is inhumanly cold, Siberian and cruel, yet he wants to spread spring. He thinks of flowers, women, *femmes-fleur*, rounded shoulders instead of military-style padded ones, flowing lines, bell-shaped skirts. He draws uninterruptedly, everywhere, sometimes making hundreds of sketches in a single day.

Clothes like architecture. Clothes like the figure eight, like tulips, like the letter *A*. Clothes that not only love women, but also make them love themselves, give them happiness. He adopts the motto "*Je maintiendrai,*" "I will maintain." Does he realize that from now on all he touches will turn into gold?

The world is stricken by poverty, scrawny and fearful, focused on ration cards and clothing coupons. Christian's whole being is in revolt, he wants to explode in purple and taffeta, interpret reality in the light of a newly cut diamond. Soon he will bring out his visions in silk, already dyed the right shade at the thread stage, never as woven fabric.

By February 13, he is a household name worldwide. A show, a press release, 24 hours — that's all it takes. Women queue to have their measurements taken and noted down in his boutique. Olivia de Havilland, the film star, purchases the model Passe-Partout in navy-blue wool. Rita Hayworth orders the evening dress Soirée for the premiere of *Gilda*. Even the queen of bohemia, Juliette Gréco, wants to wear Dior in the Quartier Latin. Ordinary women are seduced too. Despite the shortage of cloth, plagiarized versions are swiftly produced for the ordinary shops; at home, skirts are lengthened, and coats altered to have nipped-in waists.

Pale sea pearls, the collected amount of light they reflect.

The sound of sharp scissors snipping threads. *Révolution!*

London

The British are tired. Tired of the Zionists' bombs and acts of terrorism; of keeping the Arabs happy; of the fact that £80 million has been squandered in Palestine over the last two years, and that 100,000 British men are obliged to be there, far from their homes and work.

All "for the sake of a senseless, squalid war with the Jews in order to give Palestine to the Arabs, or God knows who," as Winston Churchill puts it.

Britain, which once occupied the region to secure trade routes and colonial power, no longer wants the future of Palestine to be seen as an internal British matter, but instead places the responsibility on the rest of the world. On February 18, five days after Christian Dior's dream fireworks, the British announce that they are handing the issue of Palestine's future over to the UN without making any recommendations whatsoever. They want to distance themselves from the mess, to get as far away as possible from the burden of sorting it out.

Only a few months earlier, the Arab League had considered putting forward the same proposal — to hand the whole problem over to the UN — but now Britain's stance arouses outraged protests. While Egypt, Syria, the Lebanon, Iraq, Transjordan, and Saudi Arabia have different positions, they are, above all, influenced by one man: Haj Amin al-Husseini. He is the leader of the Palestinian Arabs and holds two high positions, being both President of the Supreme Muslim Council and Grand Mufti of Jerusalem. The British are tired of him as well.

The UN decides to set up a committee comprising representatives of neutral countries. They will solve the problem. In the Arab League's view, there is no need for any committee; all that needs to be done is to establish an independent Palestinian state taking up the whole region, and everything will be sorted. Australia proposes delegates from 11 countries. The Arab League proposes that there should be a representative from each of its member countries, but the proposal is rejected. As is the Zionists' demand that the British and the Americans take part in the deliberations. Apart from Australia, the new committee comprises delegates from Canada, Czechoslovakia, Guatemala, India, Iran, the Netherlands, Peru, Sweden, Uruguay, and Yugoslavia. No one is particularly satisfied.

The Zionists demand that the Committee visit the camps in Europe where the survivors of the genocide are assembling. The Arab countries protest, arguing that it should confine itself to investigating the situation on the ground, within the existing borders of Palestine. But the UN brief states that the Committee may work exactly where it wishes, in Palestine or any other suitable location.

Emil Sandström, a Swedish lawyer, is appointed chairman, and after a first meeting in New York the Committee's members decide to spend five weeks in Palestine in the coming summer. They have a few months to carry out their task. And then, the conflict must be resolved.

Chicago

Simone de Beauvoir is forever making notes on other women's appearance. "She's very ugly." "She's beautiful, but stupid." "She's the only woman I consider intelligent enough to spend time with, but she's ugly." This is how she comments on her female acquaintances in literary Paris. Now she has left her well-marked territory and flown out to the United States for a four-month lecture tour. In the first few days, she is intensely absorbed in the experience of changing reality, becoming an outsider.

"My presence is a borrowed presence. There is no room for me on these pavements. This world, where I have made a surprising appearance, has not been waiting for me. It was complete without me — it is complete without me. It is a world where I am not, and I grasp it in my own absence."

A woman friend said she ought to visit Nelson Algren in Chicago. Simone de Beauvoir takes this advice. On February 20, she meets the writer Algren for the first time. He is 38; she is a year older.

One evening he shows her his world, the district around West Madison Street, which he calls Chicago's "lower depths." Lodging houses for single men, hostels, sleazy bars. A little band is playing in the first bar; women are stripping, making obscene movements under signs saying dancing is forbidden. They stop, listen; drunken people dance. Simone watches and says, "It's beautiful."

Nelson is surprised but pleased. "You French can see that ugliness and beauty, the grotesque and the tragic, good and evil, exist side by side," he says. "Americans can't. For them it's either one thing or the other."

The two go on to a bar frequented by black people, then to another. The streets are empty, cold, snowy, abandoned. They kiss in the taxi home.

The next day, de Beauvoir and Algren wander around the poor, dirty Polish quarter where he grew up, and where he has spent much of his adult life. Again, they go from bar to bar, chilled by a bitterly cold wind, and warm themselves up with vodka. They don't want to separate, but are obliged to; de Beauvoir has a dinner appointment with two Frenchmen whom she hates for preventing her from wandering around with Algren. When she leaves Chicago the next day, she rings him from the station, talking for as long as she can before the train departs.

"They had to take the telephone away from me by force."

On the journey to Los Angeles, she decides to return.

Nelson Algren lives in a hovel without a bathroom or fridge, in an alley full of stinking garbage bins and discarded newspapers. Simone de Beauvoir finds the poverty refreshing. The only thing that concerns her is pain. If it already hurts to leave him, how will it be if they meet again?

Simone puts this question to Nelson in a letter. He replies, "Too bad for us if another separation is going to be difficult." Come back.

Ismailia

Listing what Hasan al-Banna loathes is simple. Sexual license. Women's emancipation. Democracy. Music. Dance. Singing. Foreign influences.

From an early age, it became al-Banna's aim to prescribe what was right and to proscribe what was wrong. As an adolescent in the town of Al-Mahmudiyyah, he and some of his comrades formed a group whose mission was to improve morality through prayer and vigilance. One day, strolling along the banks of the Nile, he saw a carved wooden figure of a naked woman, at the very spot where local mothers fetched water. Some of the shipbuilders employed at the port had been amusing themselves, or had had a go at creating female forms, and young Hasan al-Banna realized there was something forbidden here to be reported, and was quick to do so. He contacted the police, and was subsequently praised in school for setting a good example.

Is this true? Did it actually happen? No matter whether it really did, it is a story that will come to play a decisive role in the development of Islam as a political movement: the often-repeated legend of the young man who was not afraid to tell the truth or correct his elders.

At 20, al-Banna lived in a house in the city of Ismailia. The rooms on the ground floor were rented by Jews, there were Christians on the first floor, and he and some friends rented the rooms at the top: a metaphor for the development of the monotheistic religions, he summarized. After this, he founded the Muslim Brotherhood.

The Netherlands

There are no tulips in bloom, the gardens have been emptied — everything has been dug up. But what were people supposed to do? Boiled tulip bulbs are said to taste much like chestnuts, bland and slightly sweet, though more than four will poison you.

One cannot speak of national scars after the war; national paralysis is more accurate. There are hardly any trains, given the lack of locomotives. The Nazis handed them over to Romania. They also dismantled much of the telephone network, so people now have to use temporary lines — at least, if they can afford it. Those who pay most are put through first. The Dutch are not allowed to buy more bulbs either, at least not for private use. Professional growers are the only ones filling the fields, as the country's entire reserve of flowers is set aside for export to the United States. The gardens remain as they are, flowerless: emptied stores.

And no one even wants to hear the word "Germany," so strong is their hatred after the Occupation. Under a new law, 25,000 Dutch nationals of German ancestry are branded "hostile subjects" and sentenced to deportation — even if they happen to be Jews, liberals, or opponents of the Nazis.

The violence takes a well-trodden path. The Dutch-Germans are given an hour to pack everything they can carry, up to a maximum of 110 pounds, then they are dispatched to jails, or to prison camps near the Dutch–German border to await deportation. Their homes and businesses are confiscated by the state. Operation Black Tulip.

And then? Relief? A sense of purity?

Ansbach, southern Germany, the American zone

Europe is full of children whose parents have been shot, gassed, tortured or starved to death, or allowed to die of cold. The children were left behind and survived — because their hair was dyed blond and they were given false Christian birth certificates; because they were placed in monasteries or convents, they crouched down in buckets inside privies, they were kept shut in behind walls, in an attic, or under a floor; or because their parents pushed them further back in the queue while they were waiting to be shot on a Danube quayside.

Some of these thousands of children are gathered together in temporary children's homes or foster homes, others drift around in loose gangs living on the streets and in the ruins. And then there are those who survived the war together with one of their parents, like Joszéf.

Hordes of children — do they share the dream of a country of their own? Maybe. They have to go somewhere, at any rate.

In a former sanatorium in Strüth, three miles north of Ansbach, UNRRA, the United Nations Relief and Rehabilitation Administration, is setting up a children's home in cooperation with the Jewish Agency, a Zionist organization. The low, white buildings provide a temporary home for some of the orphans from eastern and central Europe, until such time as they are granted authorization to travel to Palestine.

Behind the buildings lie fields where they can grow vegetables. There is a main building for UN staff and a side building where a small sick bay can be set up. Here, the skinny youngsters are to receive 3,000 calories a day, plus schooling, including lessons in Hebrew and Jewish culture.

The first group of Hungarian children arrive at the Strüth camp with the kibbutz movement Hashomer Hatzair. To begin with, their leaders want nothing to do with UNRRA or the adjoining military base, demanding that they be left to organize themselves. The camp staff have a hard job convincing them that a degree of cooperation may be beneficial to the children's health, cleanliness, and education. UNRRA promises to liaise with the military base which is loaning the buildings, and to refrain from interfering with the movement's political orientation. A calm of sorts is established for a few days, until the leaders of the kibbutz movement realize that a further 220 children are expected from Hungary. At this point, protests erupt. The leaders are seriously worried; the expected group is too big, the camp will be overpopulated, epidemics will break out. But the worst thing of all is the threat of a bad moral influence. The new group will teach the disciplined Hashomer Hatzair children to steal, smoke, refuse to obey, and refuse to work.

UNRRA's staff write anxiously to the head office in New York. They have long discussions with the kibbutz leaders about the importance of sharing responsibility for refugee issues, and about how they cannot turn their backs on a single orphaned child. But nothing helps. It is not until the leaders of Hashomer Hatzair, a socialist movement, discover that the group on its way also belongs to the kibbutz movement — albeit to the rival branch, Habonim Dror, which is not as socialist in its ideology — that they accept the situation.

Joszéf is ten. He was once called György, like his father. But when his mother handed him over to Habonim Dror, he was given a new name as a sign of his new future. Now he leaves Budapest on a journey to Palestine, with the Strüth children's refugee camp as a staging post.

It is a long way. For the last leg of the journey, from Ainring, Joszéf and the others spend over 12 hours in a lorry. They are cold and hungry when they arrive, but in surprisingly good spirits, according to reports by UNRRA staff.

The well-brought-up children from Hashomer Hatzair welcome the children from Habonim Dror with songs. Following them into the white buildings, they show them around the dormitories, the lavatories, and the refectory. They serve food and wash up afterward. It is not until two o'clock in the morning that the lights go out in the dormitories, and all the orphans, their kibbutz leaders, and the UN staff can get to sleep.

Joszéf's group arrives shockingly badly dressed from Budapest, their shoes falling apart and their garments ill fitting, with no change of clothes. Only a few children have socks. Some of them have to stay in bed until their clothing has been washed and mended. However, they do appreciate the importance of cleanliness. Their first request on the day after their arrival is to be allowed to wash.

When a third group arrives at the white buildings in Strüth a few days later, the Zionist camp is full. It contains 290 children, some of them just two years old. Around 30 of the children are about ten, like Joszéf. Just over 70 children are aged between 12 and 13, while the majority are between 14 and 16. Most of them are from Hungary, but there are also Polish children, and a few who have grown up in Yugoslavia or Russia.

Nothing is straightforward. The two competing Zionist movements demand that sick children be put into separate sick bays, so they are not contaminated by the wrong political ideology. UNRRA's staff mediate, and gradually daily life in the camp in the green German countryside becomes calmer.

There he is, then, the boy. Once he was a Hungarian, György, who lived with his mother and father in the metropolis of Budapest. Now, as the Zionist pioneer Joszéf, he's learning

Hebrew and the importance of growing crops and being a good comrade. He has lessons in reading, writing, and arithmetic, but also in singing, drama, and drawing. He gets to box in his free time. He meets the American soldiers from the camp in Ansbach who drive up in their jeeps, and on one or two rare occasions they let him take the wheel himself. There is no ignition key; you start the motor by pressing a button. It's all very interesting. Shmuel, Pinhas, and Dov, plus Dina and Miriam, are his best friends. Everything's fine.

UNRRA is responsible for assisting and rehabilitating Jewish refugees in the region, irrespective of their political activities. A UN employee summarizes the situation in a document headed *General Observations and Recommendations: the Jewish Situation in Central and Eastern Europe*:

> The Jews who remain in Europe are of two major groups. Some, and these are chiefly members of Kibbutsim, are well organized and have an ideal and a goal — Palestine, their nation, their home. Their leadership is good, their discipline excellent, their standards high. The other group still carries in its veins the poison that Hitler has brewed. They refuse to work. They steal. They engage in black market activities. Life for them is a day-to-day existence. Their aim is to get everything they can from the Germans or other enemies, to repay just a little of the humiliation and suffering that they endured for so long. If one talks to individuals, they admit they are hurting themselves but the answer is always, "When I get to Palestine — or the United States — or to England, then I shall be different."

The report notes that it is precisely the self-destructive refugees, poisoned by their experiences, who "must be served by the best personnel UNRRA can corral. There must be understanding and sympathy — firmness and tact ... [They must have] good food ... housing that permits one to share a room with one's friends — not a drab barrack filled with ... raw, wooden beds that recall the tortures of the concentration camp every moment of the day." Evil is to be exorcised by good.

Kiev

Mikhail was a sergeant and just 22 years old when he was called to the great General Zhukov. Thanks to his invention, the Red Army was able to calculate the exact number of shots fired by a weapon. As a reward and a token of the General's appreciation, Mikhail was given — what else? — a watch.

The year was 1941. General Zhukov would lead the Soviet Union to victory over the Fascists, but at the time this meeting took place, Operation Barbarossa had not yet got under way, the pact between Stalin and Hitler was still intact. And it goes without saying that the watch has disappeared. Only the myth remains.

Germany

Never again, never again, never again. These words have echoed for nearly two years, from the first day of the German capitulation in May 1945, until the last name is signed under the peace treaty, on February 10, 1947, in Paris.

On this day, the Second World War is formally at an end.

For two years, the Soviet Union, France, Great Britain, and the US have been dealing with victory, prisoners, obligations, and responsibility. They have to show people that the right side won, that democracy is superior to authoritarianism. The aim is to de-Nazify, demilitarize, decentralize, and democratize Germany. Crimes must be punished. Wounds must be healed. Events that are so far preserved only in the memories of individuals must be recognized as criminal acts and brought to justice.

The four victorious powers agree that the Nazis must be brought to account. But do they want to exact vengeance? To receive compensation? To secure peace? All of those things — but also to emphasize certain events and avert their gaze from others, both call a halt and move on.

The story of the war is not yet written. No historians have gone through the archives that were left behind. The account of the Nazi dictatorship provided by the legal proceedings will be the first overarching description. The process of law is to be a history lesson, a means to collect facts, and proof that justice has won the day.

On October 20, 1945, the International Military Tribunal took its seat at the Nuremberg Palace of Justice. What has become known as the Nuremberg trial was the first of a total of 13 trials held there. Twenty-four high-ranking Nazi leaders were charged with crimes against peace, war crimes, and crimes against humanity, as well as with murder, extermination, enslavement, deportation and persecution on political, racial, or religious grounds, and conspiracy to commit these crimes.

Journalists filled the cramped courtroom with its dark wooden paneling. For much of the time, they were bored.

The proceedings were complicated, held in four languages — the interpreting adding to the duration — and the arraigned mass-murderers looked just like any other men. Yet decisive information about the Nazi ideology nevertheless filtered out to the world, to those who had not yet understood, to those who, not having been affected, had not been concerned, and — perhaps — to those who had so far refused to believe.

Never before had crimes committed by a state been brought before a court of law, never before had responsibility been established for a nation's acts, and never before had crimes ordered by a head of government been articulated and brought to a courtroom.

Under the leadership of the chief prosecutor, Robert H. Jackson, the US lawyers sought to prove that the Nazis had both conspired to achieve world domination and engaged in a war of aggression. The lawyers also applied the idea that the defendants were representatives; according to their analysis, Hitler's regime was based upon Nazism, militarism, and economic imperialism, and representatives of each element of this unholy trinity were now to be charged.

Justice Jackson had great ambitions. The verbatim record of the trial and the final document were to be vital historic documents. For this reason, he did not wish to hear a particularly large number of witnesses. The Nazis' own documents constituted sufficient proof, and were preferable to the accounts of traumatized, self-contradicting individuals whose memories would crumple without warning when they were under cross-examination. Only a few witnesses appeared.

Twelve of the men, including Hermann Göring, Hans Frank, Alfred Rosenberg, and Julius Streicher, were sentenced to death. Three were sentenced to life imprisonment, four received custodial sentences of up to 20 years, and three were released. One of the defendants, Martin Bormann, had not been caught, while another, Gustav Krupp, being senile and seriously ill, went unpunished. After the first major sentence in the first major trial, a further 12 trials were scheduled in Nuremberg itself, and hundreds more in every country that had been subjected to Nazi occupation.

The purpose of the legal proceedings is to reconstruct the events of the recent past, by scrutinizing those documents that escaped destruction, and through cross-examinations full of lies. Yesterday's vanquished reality is to be reconstituted by means of law.

This whole process is subject to powerful political forces. It is politicians that make sure funds are earmarked for the complex tasks of finding competent legal staff, collecting evidence, coordinating investigations among the four victorious powers, ensuring equal treatment — in short, establishing a common legal basis for lawyers from four nations. And it is political forces that will soon — very soon — call off the trials.

Ideological issues leave their stamp both on the charges brought and on the descriptions of the crimes committed. Like a watermark, visible only in a given light, they set their seal on the lawyers of the nations concerned.

The Soviet Union accuses the guards from the concentration camp of Sachsenhausen of being instruments of capitalist monopoly. Since the Russian lawyers regard all the victims who died as martyrs of Fascism, there is no recognition of the specific fate suffered by the Jews in the camps, just as there is no recognition of the fate of homosexuals or Roma.

France concentrates on the victims from among the French Resistance, and avoids focusing on the many French nationals who collaborated with the Nazis. Both the Soviet Union and France lay great emphasis on their own suffering, their own resistance, and their own sacrifices when they present their cases. Thus are memories created and nations' self-images reconstructed. Memory gaps are established.

In the courtroom, the description of war, crime, and sacrifice is reduced from what probably happened to what can be proven. What most likely happened is brushed aside. The first narrative about Nazi rule takes shape. Reality is sifted through legal texts, charges, and trials, then through the reporters covering the trials. The narrative diverges, taking different directions; emphases shift. Certain aspects of historical events remain unarticulated, while other aspects are represented in the light of postwar reality.

Buchenwald and Dachau, for instance. As it is US soldiers who liberate them, these two camps become the primary symbols of Nazi cruelty in the eyes of the American public. Other camps — other types of cruelty, other ways of murdering, and other victims — are consigned to obscurity, and disappear.

Bergen-Belsen is the only camp liberated by British troops. The camp commandant, Josef Kramer, is captured there with a number of his lieutenants, and they are brought to trial promptly in the British zone in 1945. The fact that Kommandant Kramer also committed crimes during his time as *Lagerführer* at Auschwitz is included among the charges, yet the trial is called the Belsen trial, and he himself is dubbed the Beast of Belsen. International press reports on the trial barely mention Auschwitz.

Kramer's trial takes the form of a military tribunal. The legislation invoked is such that only war crimes and crimes committed against nationals of the Allied countries fall within its remit. Whatever crimes Kommandant Kramer and his subordinates have perpetrated against German nationals or nationals of other Nazi-occupied countries, they cannot be charged with them here. The fact that Josef Kramer was in charge of the extermination camp of Auschwitz–Birkenau, and that he was Kommandant Rudolf Höss's right-hand man during the period when 400,000 Hungarian Jews were murdered in the spring of 1944, is set aside. No point of the charges refers to the murder of Jews. In Great Britain, Belsen comes to symbolize the evils of Nazism.

Now, two years after the end of the war, British enthusiasm for the war trials is on the wane. The British simply cannot afford the cost. And political priorities are beginning to intervene. In the ideological power struggle that is starting to emerge between the Soviet Union and the US, views of Germany are changing. There is no specific date, no specific point in time when the focus shifts from dealing with the past to dealing with the future. Just this year, 1947 — when everything is in a vibrating state of flux, without stability and without goals, as all possibilities are still open.

Perhaps the time has come, the British reason, to stop dismantling the German nation? Maybe something besides guilt and punishment is needed? Maybe memory, the writing of history, and justice for the victims are no longer matters of preeminent importance? Rather than a severely punished Germany, Europe needs a more-or-less functioning Germany, as a shield and bulwark against the spread of Communism.

This is why the British occupation of Germany is given a new objective this year. The country is to become "stable and productive." The focus shifts to reconstruction, and to identifying future potential rather than the failings and crimes of the past. Consequently, the British decide to reduce the number of prosecutions.

The ex–Prime Minister, Winston Churchill, is one of the war trials' most forceful critics. He wants to draw a distinction between Wehrmacht soldiers and the ideologically driven SS troops. The Wehrmacht was doing its job. Sometimes it was ugly, bloody, and vile, but such is the nature of war. And Churchill contributes to a collection for the defense of General Manstein, a German general now in captivity.

What is not said in court dissipates into silence. The Nazis' persecution and murder of homosexuals does not even constitute grounds for prosecution, and is not part of the trials. The killing of Roma people is mentioned by some of the leading Nazis, but no Roma witnesses are called upon to testify. Although about 650,000 Polish Jews and an unknown number of Roma were murdered in Bełżec and Sobibór, neither death camp is mentioned even once in the course of the 13 Nuremberg trials. The death camp of Treblinka is referred to in passing on one occasion, when it is described as a concentration camp. The fate of the Jews passes in a black flash, but the racial hatred that forms the core of Nazi ideology is not one of the main issues. Rather, it is Nazi Germany's aggression, striving for world domination, and crimes against peace that dominate.

Upon the quagmire of oblivion, the world rebuilds itself.

London

On Tuesday, February 18, Great Britain relinquishes responsibility for Palestine.

On Thursday, February 20, the Prime Minister, Clement Attlee, announces that the British will be granting India independence.

On Friday, February 21, the Americans are informed that Great Britain will no longer be supporting Greece and Turkey as it did in the past.

The Empire is collapsing. The country that once wielded world dominion is relinquishing it; the country that commanded the seas and the trade routes, held the balance of power, and disseminated its language, sport, arms, education system, currency, and soldiers across the globe is now cutting ties and turning in on itself.

An incomprehensible week.

Budapest

The purge of anti-Communist elements starts on February 25 with the arrest of Béla Kovács, leader of the small farmers' party, FKGP. He is accused of conspiracy against the Soviet occupation power and sentenced to spend the rest of his life in Siberia.

He is the first, but not the last.

MARCH

Hollywood

Billie Holiday is in Hollywood to film *New Orleans.*

She plays the singing maid who falls in love with a musician, played by Louis Armstrong. Holiday both wants the role, and doesn't want it. There is an inherent humiliation in being cast as a servant, something she's spent her whole life escaping from.

She makes her first appearance 11 minutes into the film. Wearing a black dress, a white apron, and a white cap — the uniform of subordination — the maid has stolen a moment at the family's grand piano and is singing to herself. When she is caught by the white lady of the house, she receives a sharp reprimand:

> Didn't I tell you not to let me catch you at that piano again?
>
> I'm sorry, ma'am ...
>
> That music you were playing, what was it?
>
> ... It was a kind of little old blues tune.
>
> Blues? Do you play the blues only when you're blue?

No, ma'am. They just call it blues. We play it when we're blue or when we're happy. Even when we're in love.

Billie Holiday is furious with her agent, who arranged the contract. It might all have been so different. *New Orleans* could have been a film overflowing with jazz, with music as both language and content.

They shoot scene after scene. Billie Holiday's songs include the title song "Do You Know What It Means to Miss New Orleans" and "The Blues Are Brewin'." Louis Armstrong was one of her earliest heroes. Now they work together, and both his big band and his ragtime band are playing. So is Woody Herman's orchestra, with some of the country's top jazz musicians. Everything's swinging. Yet scene after scene is cut.

The director, Herbert Biberman, has caved in to pressure from the studio, RKO, which thinks there are far too many African Americans in the film. You might even get the impression that they were the ones who invented jazz.

Ansbach, southern Germany, the American zone

Joszéf is in his classroom when someone suddenly interrupts the lesson and asks him to come out into the corridor. His mother, Lilly, is waiting there.

By this time, he has spent a year in the Zionist children's home for orphans in Strüth, Ansbach. He is an exception, an anomaly, one of the few children who still have a surviving parent. The boy who always felt like the odd one out — even here, he doesn't get to be part of the majority.

The children's home provides comradeship and equality. One of the leaders is a young man called Kenedi, another is a young woman called Kati. Joszéf is very fond of them. Everything is fine, warm, and secure. His mother sent him here — but now, all of a sudden, she's standing in the corridor.

Joszéf and his mother have survived. There are four reasons for that, there are a thousand reasons, yet none suffices as an explanation.

Lilly speaks fluent German. That is one reason.

Adolf Eichmann, Nazi Germany's chief official responsible for Jewish matters, is another. When the time came to murder Hungary's Jews, he followed Reinhard Heydrich's instructions to "comb the country from west to east." Jews living in rural areas were the first to be captured, while those living in the capital were granted a few extra weeks of life.

The third reason is Stalin and his Red Army. They made their way into Budapest neighborhood by neighborhood, liberating the city from German and Hungarian Nazis one street at a time. Then they rolled in in their tanks, big red stars on green-painted metal. A beautiful sight, those tanks, the boy would think for the rest of his life. The most beautiful tanks anyone has ever seen.

The fourth reason is something else. Sometimes there is quite simply no rational explanation for why one person dies and another survives, not in the context of genocide, not in a war. Words like "luck" and "miracle" are nothing but embellishments, euphemisms for circumstances that defy comprehension. No one can establish which is hardest, to die or not to die; no one can calculate the cost of surviving, the irregular installments of guilt to be paid off.

Joszéf's father has disappeared. His aftershave a cloud of scent in memory. On the registration form for the children's home in Strüth, someone has written: "Died while carrying out forced labor in the Ukraine." And: "Mother on her way to Palestine."

Lilly sent Joszéf to this place, but now she's here all of a sudden. In her handbag she has some Hungarian sausages, and now she asks him about his future, right in the middle of a lesson.

Has she traveled all the way from Hungary to the American zone of occupied Germany with sausages in her luggage?

Does Joszéf want to stay with the children in the camp? She tells him she has remarried. Does he want to come back to Budapest with her and have a stepfather? They stand in the corridor. Does he want to follow the Zionists to Eretz Israel? Joszéf loves the taste of the Hungarian sausages, with chunks of white fat and the bold red color of paprika. Joszéf is always hungry.

Berlin

"The sign of our times is ruins," writes the German author Hans Werner Richter in his magazine *Der Ruf*. "The ruins surround our lives. They line the streets of our cities. They are our reality ... They are the outward symbol of the inner insecurity of the people of our age. The ruins live in us, as we in them. They are our new reality, which is asking to be re-shaped."

In the middle of Berlin stands the most dreaded of buildings, damaged by bombing, its windows black with forfeited power. Bricks tightly aligned, impenetrable. Small were those who entered: small, and soon dead. This was Gestapo headquarters: 8, Prinz-Albrecht-Straße.

Four flights up are the Gestapo's archives: 8 or maybe 9 million sheets of paper. Two tons of documents in total. There, and in the surrounding ruins of Berlin, a dozen US lawyers are engaged in excavating, sorting, and analyzing document after document, fact after fact, crime after crime. If trials are to be held, if there is to be any chance of justice, these must be based on evidence. And so they search methodically through the remains of Nazi Germany's meticulously constructed administrative cathedral.

It is spring in Berlin. A young lawyer, Benjamin Ferencz, has been tasked with preparing for the forthcoming war trials to be held in the American zone. At some point during these days, a member of his staff drops in at the office, a Swiss who has combed through the section of the German Foreign Office located near Tempelhof. It turns out that he has found documents no one knew existed. Precise notes, page after page, as if committed to paper by the most exacting auditor: a detailed set of accounts of the number of murders on Soviet territory of Jews, Roma, members of the resistance movement, mentally ill people, men, women, and children. *Reports on events in the Soviet Union.*

Benjamin Ferencz begins to read the daily notes made by the four *Einsatzgruppen*, A, B, C, and D, beginning on June 22, 1941, when the Nazis invaded the Soviet Union. He has a little calculator on the table in front of him. He tots up the figures. When the sum exceeds one million murdered people, he stops and travels down to Nuremberg to talk to his boss, Brigadier General Telford Taylor. There has to be a further Nuremberg trial.

The initial answer is no. Not only is there a lack of funds and available lawyers, the Pentagon has set limits on what postwar justice can cost. Nor is there popular support for more trials. People long to move on. But Benjamin Ferencz points to the newly discovered reports. The documents are unequivocal.

"We can't let these guys go."

Brigadier General Telford Taylor gives in, on condition that Benjamin Ferencz himself takes on the role of prosecutor. Ferencz is 27 years old and has never presided over a court case before. Now he is initiating the world's biggest murder trial.

Los Angeles

If Simone de Beauvoir falls head over heels in love with Nelson Algren, there is no sign of it in the letters about her travels she writes home to Jean-Paul Sartre. She has traveled on to the American west coast to give lectures on morality and existentialism, and is staying with friends.

This Thursday, March 13, she writes to Jean-Paul from a terrace in Los Angeles, well supplied with cigarettes and martinis, looking out over eucalyptus trees to the ocean. The Californian sky is a magnificent blue. Here she is, she writes, in the superficial, easygoing American world, like a queen; real life and Jean-Paul, in whom she has complete trust, are back home in France. The chasm between her American existence and her real life in Paris is vast, an oceanic trench.

"It would be almost painful if I didn't have such a strong feeling, my dear love, that we are as one, and that at the beginning of May you'll be just as I left you."

She barely mentions Nelson Algren. He only makes a marginal appearance, as an item of information dropped in carelessly in passing, at the end of the letter: "My Chicago friend has sent me a big parcel of books, and such a nice letter that I was moved by it. I can't get over the kindness of people on all sides."

Delhi

Well, you see, Dickie is cousin to Bertie — His Majesty King George VI, that is. Moreover, he is the brother of Louise, the future Queen of Sweden, and it is likely that India's ruling princes respect royal blood. He is also a good friend of Noel Coward and Winston Churchill, and has just made the acquaintance of Jawaharlal Nehru, leader of the Indian National Congress party, who appreciates both his social talents and his radical views. So the British Prime Minister, Clement Attlee, asks Dickie to don the mantle of the last Viceroy of India.

Lord Louis Francis Albert Victor Nicholas Mountbatten — Dickie to his friends — accepts. Naturally, he is a polo player. In his view, the task of leading India into the next phase is analogous to the last seven minutes of a match that his team is losing. In a letter to his cousin, the King of Great

Britain — "My dear Bertie" — he summarizes the situation thus: "The last Chukka in India — twelve goals down."

In actual fact, he is preoccupied by something other than winding up the British Empire. He is keen to reestablish the family's honor after his father, the German Prince Louis von Battenberg, was ignominiously forced out of the Navy under the anti-German rules in place during the First World War. The appointment as Viceroy has come at an awkward time.

Cousin Bertie understands his dilemma. In a letter he replies that Dickie can, of course, return to the Royal Navy in two years' time, after India, but it will naturally be more difficult for him to resume his naval career after so long an absence. So Lord Mountbatten takes a fateful decision. Although the government is giving him 18 months to wind up British sovereignty in India, he is not in the least inclined to let the last chukka drag on so long. He aims to speed things up.

Now Lord Mountbatten brings together a reliable team and prepares for the journey. He needs good advice, not least on the subject of dress. They're probably a touch left wing down there, aren't they, he asks a friend. Should he perhaps wear civvies? The friend advises him against this in no uncertain terms: "You are the last Viceroy. You are royalty. You must wear your grandest uniform and all your decorations, and be met in full panoply and with all the works."

So that is what happens.

On Saturday, March 22, Lord Mountbatten and his wife and daughter step off the aeroplane at Delhi Airport and are met by red roses from the hand of Jawaharlal Nehru. The last chukka is underway.

Europe

The Nazi system is a closed system in which only certain thoughts can be articulated and violence is the currency in a universe of fear. There is no scope within this system for lapses, cracks, or discussion. It is fueled by hate.

Is the energy principle applicable here? The principle which states that energy can neither be destroyed nor created, that the total amount remains constant over time?

Johann von Leers and Per Engdahl. In all the world's archives of documents relating to the two men, there is barely a reference to this year just after the end of the war. As if 1947 had never existed, as if it were a hiatus in their lifelines. But if time is a map, we can unfold it, put pen to paper, and make a dot here, at the point where they meet, talk to one another, and separate. They then seem to vanish, like bearers of the ring in the saga which Professor John Ronald Reuel Tolkien presents to his publishers around this time.

Clues, speculations, and isolated facts relating to the pair's activities are documented in the CIA's archives, in the archives of the Swedish Security Service in Stockholm, in the Federal German archives, in Russian archives, and in Yad Vashem in Jerusalem, to mention just a few sources. As a researcher, you can approach these institutions, ask to see everything they have, fill your hands with documents, yet merely end up accumulating more questions and more fragments. It is possible to go to ground in Europe's ruins, and Johann von Leers has gone to ground. Per Engdahl is waiting silently in the shadows. Only small movements are permitted.

Energy is constant, but it takes on new forms. The meeting between von Leers and Engdahl is also a point in time from which threads stretch on into the future and at which other names appear, but the dreams are the same: a new Europe, a homogeneous section of a continent in the world. No social classes. No political parties. The individual subordinated to the collective. Authoritarian movements, with leaders who take clear-cut decisions, and in which no time is wasted on slow, unsatisfactory democratic processes. A uniform organism, harmoniously white. Europe a Nation, to quote the British Fascist leader, Oswald Mosley.

Baltimore

In the port of Baltimore lies the *President Warfield*, a stoutly built white vessel designed for pleasure cruises around Chesapeake Bay. The airy ballroom is being stripped to make space for thousands of makeshift sleeping places, one simple wooden bed after another, and life jackets are being purchased. No more drinking and dancing, no more gently down the stream. Barbed wire is wound around the railing, the ship's flanks are reinforced with metal sheeting, and structures made out of piping are put in place so the ship can spray any attackers with hot steam.

London

Documents stamped "Top Secret" are exchanged among those in charge at the Foreign Office. The Jewish Agency wants the British authorities to allow increased immigration into Palestine. Throughout Europe, people are waiting in refugee camps — confined in their yearning for life, a new life. The fact that people are being let into Palestine at the rate of just 1,500 a month will not do; the process is too slow, unsatisfactory. Humanitarian disaster and so on.

But the British will not be moved. The cons outnumber the pros. For example, the Arab leaders have just demanded a complete moratorium on Jewish immigration. The British reply is to fall back on the status quo, and since there is no protest on the Arab side they assume the established immigration quota is accepted.

Creating "serious ill-feeling between [the British and the Arab delegations to the UN] ... is a situation which we are most anxious to avoid," the Foreign Office notes after discussions with the Arab leaders. The Palestinian leaders, in particular, play a decisive role. If there is increased Jewish immigration, the Grand Mufti and his followers may react strongly.

Moreover, the British have already turned down President Truman's special request that they let 100,000 Jews into Palestine.

The Zionists from the Jewish Agency thus receive a refusal. Jewish immigration is limited to 1,500 people a month. While the Palestine problem is planted on the UN like a primed explosive charge, the British aim to lie low and keep relations with the Arab world as good as possible. Is there any link with oil imports?

"Top Secret," as stated earlier.

Ansbach, southern Germany, the American zone

Joszéf is faced by a choice between the familiar and the unknown. He can opt for a future governed by anti-religious Zionism, find a place in new collectivist ideas, in which his fatherlessness is commonplace, even goes without saying. Or the alternative: the future of going back. To the old name, the old language, the old darkness in the old rooms, a kind of loneliness in a country that is starting to turn into a Communist dictatorship. He is ten years old, and the decision is his.

Later on, he will recall this decisive moment with resigned melancholy. If the ten-year-old had known what the grown man knows, the choice might have been a different one. But now the year is 1947, and the boy's thoughts turn to the tasty Hungarian sausages his mother has brought.

He opts for Budapest.

He believes he is choosing a home country, as Budapest is the city where he grew up. Yet in fact he is choosing a hostile country, Hungary being the nation whose people wanted to murder him. His companions in the Strüth Zionist camp continue their Hebrew and sports lessons. In just three months' time they will be dispatched to the French port of Sète, where they will board the *Exodus*.

APRIL

Berlin

There is a space between yesterday and tomorrow where one can easily lose one's way. A wasteland with no safe corners, full of young Germans, those under 25. The Nazi system is all they know. Now it has ceased to exist. What's left? A void. They seem to gather there, wavering, wanting to remain immobile.

They are caught between a yesterday under Hitler, when they "never had it so good," and a tomorrow that might turn out to be different, and might be better. But there are no guarantees.

The space cannot be located on any geographical map. Yet it clearly lies between East and West, the points of the compass are clearly marked, still no one can say which direction these young people should take. A thought spreads from one to the other, morphing into a consensus: as long as they make no choice, they cannot make the wrong one.

Dearborn

Henry Ford dies on April 7, though he seems to have been in excellent health.

In the course of his life, he not only invented the principle of the production line, used to manufacture cars and war material

— something which none other than Joseph Stalin considered crucial for the Allies' victory over the Germans — but also, in the early 1920s, he funded the translation and publication in the United States of *The Protocols of the Elders of Zion*, and printed 500,000 copies.

In 1919, he bought the *Dearborn Independent* newspaper, which went on to publish a series of anti-Jewish articles. These were collected in a book called *The International Jew: The World's Foremost Problem*, together with *The Protocols of the Elders of Zion*, and one of the readers they inspired was Baldur von Schirach, later to become the leader of the Hitler Youth. A "decisive" book for his anti-Semitic development, he declared when testifying in Nuremberg. Another reader on whom it made a deep impression was Adolf Hitler; hence Henry Ford is the only American mentioned by name in *Mein Kampf.*

Although Ford made a public apology in 1927, admitting that *The Protocols of the Elders of Zion* was based on lies and forgery, in 1938 he received the highest Nazi order that could be conferred on a non-German, the Order of the German Eagle, together with a personal greeting from Adolf Hitler, who, incidentally, had a portrait of Henry on the wall of his Munich office.

Now he is dead. So it goes.

Delhi

Lord Mountbatten, the last Viceroy of India, is holding talks about the country's future with three men who can scarcely bear the sight of each another. The Earl prefers Jawaharlal Nehru, one of the leaders of the Indian National Congress. Mohandas Gandhi, on the other hand, also from the Congress party, is a person he views as a half-naked fakir, an unfathomable spiritual phenomenon, and he regards it as divine providence when their meetings fall on a Monday, the one day of the week on which Gandhi abstains from speech. The third man, Muhammad Ali Jinnah, the leader of the All-India Muslim League — well, he, in Dickie's view, is a psychopath, so chilly that one feels the cold if one spends any length of time in the same room. The three Indian leaders are all lawyers, thoroughly Anglicized, highly qualified, and educated partly in Great Britain.

Could they have been friends, or at least allies, setting aside their mutual aversion? Could they have approached the Viceroy, Dickie, in a different way? Could the bloodbath of Partition have been averted? But Dickie is in a hurry, and the three men are competing for power and influence.

Muhammad Ali Jinnah, the political leader of the Raj's Muslims, eats pork, drinks whisky, and seldom frequents the mosque. He loathes the way Gandhi brings spirituality into politics — "it is a crime to mix up politics and religion the way he has done" — and is convinced that religion fuels chauvinism among both Hindus and Muslims. For this reason, he balks at conferring any spiritual authority on Gandhi by using the title "Mahatma," the Great Soul. "Mr." will do just fine, and this is something for which Gandhi cannot forgive him. In the past, Jinnah strove to unite the Hindu-dominated National Congress and the Muslim League, but the growing violence has made him an increasingly strong advocate of partition. Now he wants to see a separate Muslim state.

But Gandhi resists all thoughts of what he calls "vivisection." He would prefer a community with the Muslim Jinnah in the leadership to seeing the body of Mother India rent asunder. Jawaharlal Nehru cannot accept Gandhi's attitude, though he too is initially opposed to partition. But when violence tears the country apart from within, his position changes. Muslims and Hindus drown each other, burn each other's houses down, and drill holes in each other's skulls to watch each other bleed slowly to death.

As mentioned, Dickie likes Nehru best. The two men agree that old Gandhi doesn't understand what's going on; he is too busy traveling around, trying, by his presence, to lay balm on open wounds. They also agree that it would be better if Jinnah were elsewhere — let him have his moth-eaten Pakistan to keep him happy.

On April 10, Lord Mountbatten gathers his staff together and announces that a just solution has been worked out. It is important that responsibility for the solution be transferred to the people of India, to avoid the blame being placed on Great Britain. By the way, Punjab and Bengal will have to be divided.

Thus Great Britain's 350-year-old Raj fractures into three fragments: East and West Pakistan — a geographically impossible unit, separated by thousands of miles — with the Indian subcontinent in between. This is how its people fall apart: villages, houses, families. This is how life itself falls apart, giving way to arson and torn-up rice paddies, migration and flight, thousands of unburied bodies along the railway lines. This is how everything falls apart.

Berlin

A predicament between no-more-war and peace. A huge mess.

While work is in progress on the seventeenth edition of *Der Ruf*, the magazine is banned. The authorities in the American zone have tired of constantly having to censor it; they might as well close the whole thing down.

The editor, Hans Werner Richter, and his staff have all been German POWs in US custody, and now they will not be confined within the thinking of the victorious powers. They want to see links between the Eastern and Western zones, rather than ever-growing gaps, and dream of socialism as a bridge between the Soviet Union and the Western powers.

All around them, front pages, articles, and public conversation are full of voices keen to redeem the German spirit, *der Geist*, from Nazism. The one has nothing to do with the other, the voices claim; it's all a malicious misunderstanding. The German spirit is essentially a rich and cultivated one, but it has been taken hostage by vile Nazism.

The circle of young writers to which Hans Werner Richter belongs are starving like everyone else; they lack employment and social position, but are ready to create a new German language free of lies. Distancing themselves from the notion of collective guilt, they are, at the same time, repelled by the sanctimonious attitude now spreading through Germany, which they liken to snails' slime.

The writer Thomas Mann also observes the attempts under way in his former home country to mask the violence of the last 14 years with the notion that German culture is essentially good. He has just completed a novel that depicts a composer who, entering into a pact with the devil to acquire great new artistic knowledge and success, has to forfeit his capacity for love in exchange. The novel arises from the understanding that the bourgeois culture in which Mann lived, and loved, held the embryo of Nazism within. The idea of intoxication merges with that of anti-reason, he notes. The result is the tragic fate of Germany.

Jura

One bright cold day in April, the clock strikes 13. Eric Arthur Blair steps ashore on the Scottish isle of Jura with his three-year-old son, Richard, and that is just about all he brings. His wife, Eileen, died during a routine operation less than a year after they had adopted the boy. Now only father and son are left.

Eric Blair is worn out and poor, and does what he can to keep his grief at bay. Since Eileen's death, he has been writing as though possessed: book reviews, essays, reportage, analyses. A friend at *The Observer* lends him his house on Jura, and Blair gratefully accepts the opportunity to leave the world to itself.

To reach the whitewashed house in Barnhill, a good six miles from Ardlussa, you take the "Long Road" northward until it comes to an end, then continue a little further. There stands the house, as luminously white as a tranquilizer. And below it, the sea. Nothing more, nothing else. That is all. House. Sky. Heath. Sea.

He spent some time in Barnhill last year. Now he notes in his diary that nothing is the same, everything is in disarray. The grass hasn't started to grow yet, there are hardly any birds to be seen, the hares are few and far between. On April 12, the sea is calm. No seals in sight.

We speak of time as a flow, a broadly meandering river that one cannot step into twice; we say it forms loops, yet flows onward. As if it issues from a spring, has a direction and an ocean waiting somewhere.

Sometimes there are people who place themselves in the middle of the metaphor, turning themselves into measuring instruments and analysts. What direction are we flowing in, what is the destination toward which blood is coursing, and what are people doing with their thoughts? What words are used, and what is the meaning they are designed to conceal?

Eric Blair is one of them. On Jura, with its white rabbits and adders, he takes as clear and unsentimental a view of the surrounding reality as of the surrounding language. As George Orwell, he writes:

> In our time, political speech and writing are largely the defense of the indefensible. Things like the continuance of British rule in India, the Russian purges and deportations, the dropping of the atom bombs on Japan, can indeed be defended, but only by arguments which are too brutal for most people to face, and which do not square with the professed aims of the political parties. Thus political language has to consist largely of euphemism, question-begging and sheer cloudy vagueness. Defenseless villages are bombarded from the air, the inhabitants driven out into the countryside, the cattle machine-gunned, the huts set on fire with incendiary bullets: this is called *pacification*.

> Millions of peasants are robbed of their farms and sent trudging along the roads with no more than they can carry: this is called *transfer of population* or *rectification of frontiers*. People are imprisoned for years without trial, or shot in the back of the neck or sent to die of scurvy in Arctic lumber camps: this is called *elimination of unreliable elements*. Such phraseology is needed if one wants to name things without calling up mental pictures of them.

Now he is on the run from his success as an author and journalist, escaping from requests for lectures and commissions, withdrawing from the public sphere and the unusually cold winter, to live life in the Inner Hebrides. There is no electricity or running water, but he has a glass of brandy a day, an idea for his next book, and the desolate surroundings he needs to be able to realize it.

Marseille

By this time, the British are aware of the white ship that was reconditioned in Baltimore harbor and has now arrived in Marseille. In fact, they have got to know about several old vessels being used for illegal smuggling of refugees. Over the last month alone, they have prevented eight ships from mooring in Palestine, each of which was carrying about a thousand surviving prisoners from the camps. The Jews on board are taken to camps on Cyprus which are already overfull, and there they must await their lawful turn to leave.

The British call on France to take action to halt the flows of refugees from the French coast, in particular this American passenger vessel, the *President Warfield.* Make use of administrative obstacles, they write to the French Foreign Ministry, prevent the ship from restocking with food and drink, refer to maritime safety, do what the hell you like, but don't let it out of the port of Marseille.

Hundreds of thousands of people drifting through Europe, on their way out, on their way home, on their way to a place unknown, for the past is no longer a dwelling place.

Over 5,000 Jews gather at the Romanian border with Hungary. Where are they heading? Onward. The Hungarians decide to arrest all those who cross the border without legal documents and send them back to Romania.

Rumors are heard, so frequent, so worrying, and from such reliable sources that one must assume they are true. In the American occupation zone of Germany alone, over 125,000 people are making their preparations, all of them with the same goal in mind: to reach Palestine with false papers and by unlawful means.

Columbia, South Carolina

The present can be defined as a state of war-like peace.

Bernard Baruch, the American millionaire and presidential adviser, stands below the portrait of himself, giving a speech written by someone else. It is April 16. He wants to have workers working harder, fewer strikes, and agreement between labor unions and employers.

The world needs to renew itself, both physically and spiritually, says Baruch. This simple sentence is sufficiently vague to contain the universal anxiety about such renewal, mixed with the universal hope that it will actually come to pass — words like a container of inflammable gas.

"Let us not be deceived. We are today in the midst of a cold war. Our enemies are to be found abroad and at home."

The American press quotes and praises Baruch, the analysis of a cold war impresses people with its acuity, and people adopt the concept as if this were the first time it had been uttered. Yet these words are in fact taken from an essay on the atom bomb already written by George Orwell in 1945. Orwell's words capture the contemporary situation, but two years later the contemporary situation has moved on and takes the words back.

The term "cold war" quickly gains even wider currency when journalist Walter Lippmann's book of that name appears. *The Cold War* contains a series of articles in which Lippmann roundly criticizes President Truman's foreign policy and anti-Soviet strategy. The crack in the world that is widening in violence, the Cold War, actually originates with the American quest for power, as well as incompetence, says Lippmann.

He is not alone. Many heavyweight US politicians accuse America of replacing British imperialism in the Middle East with their own, risking war with the Soviet Union, abandoning important diplomatic negotiations, misunderstanding the civil war in Greece, supporting totalitarian forces there, and frightening the American people.

In his diary, President Truman makes no reference either to Lippmann or to his critique.

New York

Simone de Beauvoir dines with Marcel Duchamp on April 19. Afterward, she attends a party held in her honor. Le Corbusier is there, as are Kurt Weill and Charlie Chaplin.

Washington

Raphael Lemkin will never forget the time he heard Winston Churchill speak. The speech, broadcast by radio two months after Hitler's invasion of the Soviet Union in June 1941, dealt with what was actually happening under cover of the fairy tale name "Operation Barbarossa":

> The aggressor ... retaliates by the most frightful cruelties. As his armies advance, whole districts are being exterminated. Scores of thousands — literally scores of thousands — of executions in cold blood are being perpetrated by the German Police-troops upon the Russian patriots who defend their native soil. Since the Mongol invasions of Europe in the sixteenth century, there has never been methodical, merciless butchery on such a scale, or approaching such a scale ... We are in the presence of a crime without a name.

The words lingered. A lawyer specializing in international law, Lemkin was living in exile, having fled from the Nazis in Poland. He pondered the crime without a name, and decided to name it.

A few months before Churchill's speech, Lemkin arrived in the United States. His reputation grew thanks to the book *Axis Rule in Occupied Europe*, published in November 1944, in which he analyzed and defined the crime to which he had given the name of genocide.

After the war, he was given a job at the Pentagon examining Nazi declarations and decrees on the persecution and murder of Jews in the occupied countries. But Raphael Lemkin wanted more; he wanted to change the world.

In the name of honesty: while all this is true, it is also misleading. No human life can be reduced to individual sentences. Fragments of Lemkin's correspondence, notes, and an unfinished autobiography reveal everything else that Raphael Lemkin was. Traces of his yearning for love, and his bitterness. The warm and happy closeness to his mother, the memories of a childhood in which he embraced birch trees and rode bareback, feeling a deep sense of oneness with all living things. Here is the deep wound that will never heal: when he discovers that his mother was murdered in Treblinka. Here are his relationships with women who want to take care of him, the tenderness he inspires. The lack of clarity about his emotions. What happens to his feelings of desire? Secrets, unwritten diaries. The self-chosen solitude in which he wraps himself, the despair he breathes. And then there is the fact that will set its stamp on the rest of his life: his absolute determination, his obsession, to make genocide an internationally recognized crime.

To get closer to the power to change the world, he contacted one of the judges at the US Supreme Court, Robert H Jackson.

Lemkin sent articles about his work, and suggested that the judge borrow his book from the Supreme Court's library. Robert H Jackson read it. Later, when President Truman appointed Jackson chief prosecutor at the first Nuremberg trial, Lemkin's ideas and words filtered down into its work.

Gradually but resolutely, Lemkin approached the inner circle of lawyers working on the preparations for the trials. New laws had to be drafted. There were no old crimes in existence that covered the recent violence. Two new international offenses were defined: crimes against humanity and crimes against peace.

Through Robert H Jackson, Lemkin was invited to take part in the preparatory work, but he was not given any specific role. He made both friends and enemies. His name was penciled into the list of participants in the working group, not written in ink. He was not given an extension of his own. There were colleagues who thought him maladroit, seeing him as someone who bragged about his book and ignored those around him. Yet he made an impression. It was thanks to his intense lobbying that the concept of genocide was included in the charges against Hermann Göring, Joachim von Ribbentrop, Hans Frank, and the other Nazi leaders. And during the International Military Tribunal — the first major trial in Nuremberg — "genocide" was uttered for the first time in a courtroom. The British prosecutor even quoted verbatim from Lemkin's book during one cross-examination.

He himself endured equally in the light and the shadow. At the same time as the trial was taking place, he was trying to find out what had happened to his parents and the rest of his family.

He discovered that the US authorities in Germany were releasing 500 SS men every day, simply because they could not afford to keep them in custody. Neither photographs nor fingerprints were kept. He slept badly owing to anxiety and grief.

Unshaven, with untrimmed hair and an unkempt appearance, Lemkin wandered the corridors of Nuremberg's Grand Hotel, where the US lawyers had their quarters. A kind soul in torment, a shadow who longed to bring more light into the world. His colleagues were sympathetic, but could hardly bear his presence.

Lemkin went as far as to ask one of the prosecutors to persuade the president of the tribunal to incorporate the concept of genocide in the judgment to be handed down at Nuremberg:

> Indeed, we cannot keep telling the world in endless sentences: Don't murder members of national, racial and religious groups; don't sterilize them; don't impose abortions on them; don't steal children from them; don't compel their women to bear children for your country; and so on. But we must tell the world now, at this unique occasion, don't practice Genocide.

When the judgment was pronounced, Raphael Lemkin was on his sickbed in Paris. Several years — a war, a peace, the murder of millions of people, and a trial — had taken place since he had heard Winston Churchill refer to the crime without a name. He listened to the radio broadcast about Nuremberg, and until the judgment had been read out in full, hope remained. But there was not a word in it about genocide — nothing.

Malmö

Per Engdahl is gathering his forces: spidery networks, the old boys, diffusion of impulses.

The Swedish Security Service knows that Engdahl contacted some of the remaining European Nazi and Fascist cells back in 1945. They know he is now cooperating with Carl-Ernfrid Carlberg, the Swedish financier. This Carlberg runs a publishing house in Stockholm whose activities have included translating and publishing books by Adolf Hitler and Josef Goebbels, and publishing *The Protocols of the Elders of Zion.* During the war, Carlberg gathered information and advertised the publication of a two-volume "Who's Who of Jews in Sweden," which listed all Swedish Jews and their spouses, and was responsible for publishing the Swedish version of the Wehrmacht's propaganda magazine *Signal.*

Carl-Ernfrid Carlberg is devoted and unwavering in his Nazism. In the run-up to Hitler's fiftieth birthday, he collected money for a gift. After the news of the attempt on the Führer's life in 1939, he sent a personal telegram to wish him well.

The Swedish police know that the millionaire Carlberg is a member of Per Engdahl's Fascist movement, and that Carlberg and Countess Lili Hamilton are the instigators of the Committee to Assist the Children of Germany, and later of an organization called Assistance for German Officers. Over the years, they collect about 40 million Swedish crowns, money that benefits not only poverty-stricken German children, but also a large number of Nazi officers. Countess Hamilton later becomes vice-president of Stille Hilfe [Silent Aid], an organization that provides support for Nazis who are in hiding, sentenced, or on the run.

But as yet the Swedish police are unaware that Carlberg is in touch with Ludwig Lienhard, an SS officer who, as far back as 1944, was involved in shipping highly qualified Nazis to Argentina via Sweden. In a complex operation, in which he was acting on behalf of both the Swedish Government and Nazi Germany in parallel, it appears that he got several thousand Swedish-speaking Estonians who were at risk of Soviet reprisals out of the country, hiding them in Stockholm with Carl-Ernfrid Carlberg's assistance.

Now Lienhard wants to travel to Argentina himself, and he is funding the journey by offering space for fugitives on board an old ship, *Falken*, which is in Stockholm for repairs. The boat is in very poor condition. Carlberg is contacted; he inspects the vessel and invests at least 30,000 Swedish crowns in the project.

In the course of police interrogations later in 1947, Carlberg will plead debilitating memory loss, and do what he can to downplay the link between himself and Ludwig Lienhard. But in this cool spring, they are both visited by a young German-Argentinian, Carlos Schultz. He has been instructed by President Perón to recruit 1,000 people to come to Argentina, preferably Estonians or Swedish-speaking Estonians, but chiefly highly educated people with Aryan blood. Carlos Schultz and Ludwig Lienhard make long lists of Nazis in Sweden, and equally long lists of Danes and Norwegians known to have worked for the Nazis. The names are sent to Buenos Aires, which responds with passports and authorization to enter the country. Argentine diplomats in Stockholm and Copenhagen lend a helping hand. Passports are stolen and forged, identities are concealed.

1947

The illegal trafficking of fugitives over the border between German and southern Jutland continues: a steady stream of white, well-educated refugees, who are dispatched through Denmark to Sweden, and onward to Latin America.

MAY

Delhi

The leader of the All-India Muslim League, Muhammad Ali Jinnah, wants his Pakistan, and he wants to lead it. But in his opinion, Lord Mountbatten is forcing the process of partition ahead too fast. A meeting with a member of Lord Mountbatten's staff ends with Jinnah grasping the Briton's arm and declaring gravely that dividing the Punjab and Bengal will prove to be a huge mistake. He asks the official to convey that message to Lord Mountbatten.

In Lahore, gangs of Muslims burn down the houses of Sikhs and Hindus to drive them out. In their turn, Hindus and Sikhs gather weapons to strike back. Official reports state that 3,600 people have been murdered in the cities of Lahore and Rawalpindi since March.

If the partition of India is to be practicable and religiously orthodox, some people will either have to move, or die. Villages are raided and torched. Trains are attacked and passengers stabbed. Streams of refugees are attacked. Men are castrated. Women are abducted and raped. Women are abducted and their breasts cut off. Their noses and arms are cut off. The names of their rapists are carved into their skin. Women are abducted, at least 75,000 women, and subjected to sexual violence to weaken the group they belong to, to humiliate. Certain groups respond by killing the women themselves, before the enemy can seize them. Fathers cut their daughters', sisters', and wives' throats, or burn them to death. The wells of the Punjab fill up with corpses when women are ordered to kill themselves. In the small village of Thoha Khalsa in the district of Rawalpindi, 93 women throw themselves into the communal well. Three survive because there is not enough water to drown them all.

Partition — the way in which it is rushed through, the way in which it is implemented — forces 4.5 million non-Muslims and 5.5 million Muslims to flee in the state of Punjab alone. A total of 13 million people flee.

Later, Dickie will comment on his stint as the last Viceroy of India, responsible for the British withdrawal, with the words "I fucked it up."

New York

Simone de Beauvoir and Nelson Algren are reunited on May 10. He gives her a silver ring.

London, the House of Commons

> Major Tufton Beamish: What arrangements have been made to counter Zionist plans for the illegal emigration of Jews from Europe to Palestine?
>
> Mr. McNeil, British Minister of State for Foreign Affairs: It would clearly lessen the efficiency of the measures taken

against illegal immigration of Jews into Palestine if these measures were made public, but I hope the honorable and gallant Gentleman will accept my assurance that the measures are vigorous, extensive, and varied in character.

Major Tufton Beamish: Will the Minister say whether the arrangements are effective?

Mr. McNeil: To some degree.

Mr. Anthony Nutting: Can the Minister say what is the use of asking governments, such as has been done in the case of Italy, to stop the emigration of Jews to Palestine ... Obviously, the Italians do not want these Jews in Italy, and if they are dumped on them, surely the Minister must realize that they are only too anxious to get them out.

Jura

George Orwell is ill again. He spends three days in bed, and when he finally gets up he is trembling with weakness.

The whitewashed house on the great heath beside the endless ocean has four small bedrooms and a spacious kitchen. Orwell writes by the light of a storm lantern, chain-smoking black tobacco in cigarettes he rolls himself, filling the rooms with foggy, unhealthy smoke. Though not on top form, he keeps out of the doctor's way to avoid a diagnosis. Once he was a roving reporter; now only a battery-driven radio links him with the rest of the world.

Oilskins, silence, a kind of uneasiness in his eyes.

His sister Avril comes to Jura to look after his little son, so that Orwell can work on his book. On May 12, the air is still and warm. The wild cherry trees are in blossom.

New York

Billie Holiday is 32 years old and at the peak of her career. The girl who grew up in Baltimore, who was raped, put in a children's home, and arrested for prostitution as a 14-year-old, now earns about a thousand dollars a week from singing.

The jazz magazine *Down Beat* ranks her number two in its poll for the second year running. Success takes her from club to club, from stage to stage, from one poll to another. Billie Holiday is everywhere. She has a lover, an agent, and a dog called Mister. She has alcohol, money, and an addiction. Her agent tries to stop her drug abuse — he managed to get her into a clinic in February — but only a few weeks later she is taking drugs again. When in Hollywood to shoot *New Orleans*, her lover, Joe Guy, brings her deliveries from New York. Practically all her earnings go on heroin.

On May 24, she appears at Carnegie Hall, New York, for the second time in the year. The audience loves her performance of "There Is No Greater Love." Four days later, she is in front of a judge, charged with possessing drugs, after a police raid on her apartment. The trial is called *The United States of America v. Billie Holiday*, and that's just how she feels. With no defense attorney in place, tired, suffering from cold turkey and dehydration, she pleads guilty. On May 28, she is sentenced to a year in jail.

Cairo

Apart from Hasan al-Banna's father, the clockmaker, only a few people were at an early stage initiated into the secret of his organization, the Muslim Brotherhood.

Two key words are shared. One is well known and familiar: the *umma*. All Muslims are interlinked in a universe free of racism and oppression. This community, transcending geographic and national borders, does not separate one individual from another. In heart and soul, all Muslims are linked by ties of faith. Islam, in the creed of the clockmaker's son, is motherland and nationality in one.

The other key word has lain in a thousand-year sleep, consigned to oblivion: *jihad*.

From the very beginning, his movement has two parallel goals: social work on the one hand, and political work on the other. Goodwill and charity are the ideals associated with the one, while national independence and a state run in accordance with Islam the objectives of the other.

But the growing numbers of Jews moving to Palestine prompt the clockmaker's son to direct his gaze beyond the borders of oppressed Egypt. Hasan al-Banna declares that the Jews hate Islam, and that all Muslims, irrespective of their age and sex, are duty-bound to resist Jewish conspiracies and hatred. Jihad is introduced. The aim is to smash oppression wherever it appears, and to free the oppressed from their oppressors.

One of the people initiated at an early stage into the inner circle of the Muslim Brotherhood is Haj Amin al-Husseini, the man who holds the religious office of Grand Mufti of Jerusalem, the political leader of the Palestinian Arabs.

The Grand Mufti was declared an honorary Aryan in Nazi Germany, and Hitler's soldiers read his writings about the enemy within that had to be extirpated. He recruited at least 20,000 Bosnian Muslims to the SS. From 1941 to 1945, he lived in Berlin, met his friend Hitler, and discussed his vision of solving the Jewish problem in the Middle East in the same way as in Europe.

Hitler sympathized with his ideas and agreed. When the time was ripe, the Grand Mufti could unleash the Arab struggle against those who were occupying the Arabs' *Lebensraum* under British protection. But Hitler considered the timing to be problematic. Could the Grand Mufti wait? Maybe they then sipped lemonade together. After the meeting, Haj Amin al-Husseini noted down on the squared paper in his diary, in his regular, elegant hand, what his friend had said:

> I know your life history. I followed with interest your long and dangerous journey. I was very concerned about you. I am happy that you are with us now and that you are now in a position to add your strength to the common cause.

During his four years in Berlin, Haj Amin al-Husseini regularly contributed to German short-wave radio broadcasts targeting the Arab-speaking world, like a kind of Islamist simultaneous interpreter with a single sentence to interpret: Jews are the enemy. In 1943, he declared that the Germans had found the final solution to the Jewish plague. Hitler's Propaganda Minister, Goebbels, called the broadcasts "our long-range gun in the ether."

But it was complicated. The Grand Mufti knew the Nazis themselves had had a hand in the immigration of German Jews into Palestine. Cooperation with Zionist organizations under the Haavara Agreement had enabled 60,000 Jews to emigrate to Palestine between 1933 and 1941. This seems to have been advantageous for both Zionists and Nazis: the Jews escaped persecution, Palestine's Jewish population grew, and the Nazis gained economic benefits through the obligatory export of German goods. Haj Amin al-Husseini had condemned all this. But during the war years, ties with the Nazis grew stronger. He wrote letters to Himmler and Ribbentrop reminding them of their promises, their declaration that they would triumph together, and he called on them again and again to bomb the Jews in Tel Aviv and Jerusalem.

Haj Amin al-Husseini received both ideological and financial support from Nazi Germany and passed some of it on to his friend Hasan al-Banna.

But there were differences between the friends. When the war was over, with both Fascists and Nazis vanquished, Hasan al-Banna assumed that the very idea of a Jewish state had also been vanquished. If there was no persecution of Jews, he assumed, there would, quite simply, be no international support for such a state. In 1945, he proposed that the Allies seize the Nazis' assets and share them out among surviving Jews. This would be a way to achieve twofold justice, by punishing the criminals and compensating the victims of crime. As for the homeless Jews in Europe, they should be shipped to Australia. Alternatively, if every tenth American family were to take in one Jewish refugee, the problems of thousands of Jews would be solved.

New York

And so it is that time takes a step in a new direction, from one imaginable future to another. A few carefully chosen words, a specific moment, a hidden agenda. An unforeseeable consequence — and nothing is the same.

On May 14, the messenger is Andrei Gromyko, the Soviet representative to the United Nations. His words flash in the geopolitical darkness when he announces the Soviet Union's new stance on the future of Palestine.

Soviet policy was formerly based on the Leninist-Stalinist theory that Jews did not meet the criteria necessary to form a nation, that the Zionist movement was a bourgeois lackey serving imperialism, a product of rootless cosmopolitan Jews. But now? It is an "indisputable fact" that the Jewish people have "historical roots" in Palestine. There can be no question of any "unilateral solution" that fails to take account of "the legitimate rights of the Jewish people."

> The fact that no western European State has been able to ensure the defense of the elementary rights of the Jewish people, and to safeguard it against the violence of the fascist executioners, explains the aspirations of the Jews to establish their own State. It would be unjust ... to deny the right of the Jewish people to realize this aspiration ... particularly in view of all it has undergone during the Second World War.

No one anticipated these words. No explanation is provided. Maybe the Soviet Union wants Great Britain out of the Middle East in order to boost its own power. Maybe there are domestic political motives. But whatever the reason, everything has changed. From now on, a new future illuminates the present with a new kind of light. The shadows, too, change shape.

Warsaw

The warm weather penetrates the city's basements, which lie open, roofless, and exposed by bombs and collapsing masonry. During the war, no one had time to bury the bodies properly; there were too many, a quarter of a million dead in a single city. Now the shallow graves are inadequate. This spring, Warsaw stinks of corpses.

Paris

The flight from New York to France takes 24 hours. When Simone de Beauvoir returns to her Paris, she finds the city dull and disagreeable. She flees from it, moving into a *pension* just outside Versailles to rest, work, walk, and think of Nelson Algren.

She writes to him on May 18 with the red fountain pen he gave her, the silver ring on her finger. She has never worn a ring before. When her Parisian friends see it, they are surprised and think it very beautiful.

Simone writes that she misses him. His lips, his hands, his warm, strong body, his face, and his smile. And missing him becomes a pleasure, as the strength of her longing proves he isn't a dream. He is really there, he exists, and they will meet again.

"I am your wife forever."

New York

Great Britain makes a request to the UN, whose Secretary-General, Trygve Lie, passes it on. Would all the member states please be kind enough to prevent the refugees from traveling to Palestine?

Since 1939, 97,000 Jews have been admitted to Palestine. The current legal immigration rate is 18,000 a year, but in the last few months alone 15,000 refugees have been prevented from getting there by boat, across the Mediterranean.

Do not allow them to cross your territory; do not allow them to cross the border; do not allow their boats to leave your ports. Thank you.

JUNE

Jura

A slight mist over George Orwell's part of the isle of Jura. Dead calm at sea. He notes down the temperature of the air and the temperament of the sea, day by day. He reminds himself to buy more petrol for the generator, and to order fruit trees for the coming spring, as well as more tulip bulbs. Nothing in his daily notes suggests who he is, or what he is thinking about. Nothing even suggests that he is writing a book.

From time to time, he kills an adder. The area is full of them. Orwell is fond of telling his friends about the cigar remedy for an adder bite: you simply light a cigar and stub it out on the wound. No one believes he would actually do that himself.

Budapest

For an outsider, Budapest is a confusing place. Each encounter produces a new, contradictory version of reality. No one has the same story to tell. Existence has exploded.

Some live in fear of the secret police, who may come at any moment and drag them away. Friends and neighbors have vanished. No one ever comes back, they say. Others say the panic is exaggerated; Communists are like Russians, good and decent, and anyone who claims otherwise is "reactionary." Someone calculates that there are between 15,000 and 20,000 political prisoners in the country, while the Communist leader, Mátyás Rákosi, says they probably number a few hundred. But there is a degree of political unease, Mr. Rákosi concedes. Many Hungarians have views on the weakened position of the church and the fact that religious education has been eliminated from schools, and are voicing them. On the other hand, the nationalization of church property is seen as a good thing; the men of the cloth used to spend too much of their time farming. The Hungarian nobility have fled the country by now, or are living modest lives, doing lowly work and selling their belongings in the streets.

The middle class is gradually being ground down into a proletarian lifestyle, a special correspondent from the *Sydney Morning Herald* reports on June 3. Many people are on unpredictable blacklists and have a hard time finding work. There are more beggars than ever; war-wounded ex-soldiers without pensions fill the streets of Budapest, limping toward passersby with whispered pleas for help. Russian lorries play Soviet marches through loudspeakers. Diesel fumes, dirt, and fear. Political prisoners march through the streets, including women and children, on their way to perform penal labor.

All Budapest residents have to spend ten days a year clearing up rubbish and debris from ruined buildings, but those who can afford to bribe their way out of this duty do so. The shops are well stocked, the street lamps are lit at night, people go out to theaters and cafés, buy new hats, and eat cakes with apricot jam and cream — and they all say the same thing, like a mantra, a spell: Oh, if only we could afford to live the way we do!

Somewhere in all this, my father.

'Arab al-Zubayd

There is a limit already. Hamdeh Jom'a gives her Jewish friends presents, but they never play together. That's the way life is. And even though every path down from the hills of Galilee can fork and lead into a new one, most people take the tracks that are already well worn.

In the neighboring village lives Fifa Hadeve, Hamdeh's Jewish sister, who can both read and write. Hamdeh and Fifa are really as alike as two sisters; they call each other "blood sisters," and they are equally beautiful. Fifa is a fine horsewoman. If a man attempts to approach her, she flees by motorbike, by cycle, or on horseback, taking whatever alternative is available. She tells her sister Hamdeh to find a good husband, not just anyone.

"Find one who can read, at least. Even if he's poor, he'll make you rich. If you choose a husband for his looks today, you'll suffer tomorrow."

When Hamdeh's mother dies, Fifa comes to make sure that Hamdeh and her family are coping, that they're not short of anything, neither chickpeas nor beans. And if things had stayed the same, nothing would have changed.

One day Fifa tells Hamdeh that God has sent her a bridegroom. His father is English and his mother Jewish, and he lives in Haifa. Will Hamdeh go with her to inspect him and see if he is a good match? Hamdeh is happy to oblige, and asks her father's permission. He says no. They may be blood sisters, close friends, equally beautiful, and so on, but there is a limit, and they've reached it now.

Cambridge, Massachusetts

A virulent civil war in Greece claims life after life. The British decision, taken in February, to stop providing assistance to that grievously wounded country sets off intensive American activity. Since the end of the war, Great Britain has provided support to Iran, Turkey, and Greece, in its efforts to hold off Soviet intervention. Now President Truman determines to take the place of the British, as these countries will otherwise be left exposed and vulnerable to Stalin's harsh embrace.

Just three weeks after Britain's announcement in February, Truman stands before Congress and sets out his doctrine: America is taking over responsibility for the world.

The toughest possible resistance must meet *Tovarish* Stalin and his ideology. Communism must be opposed. Can Congress grant $400 million for Turkey and Greece?

One thing leads to another. A heated debate follows this articulation of the Truman Doctrine, and an idea occurs to Secretary of State Marshall. On June 5, he gives a speech at Harvard University, and the globe turns a further degree toward the future we call now.

> The truth of the matter is that Europe's requirements for the next three or four years of foreign food and other essential products — principally from America — are so

> much greater than her present ability to pay that she must have substantial additional help or face economic, social, and political deterioration of a very grave character.

He proposes that the US provide an emergency package of $5 billion, to be invested in 16 countries for four years. In one fell swoop, the US has a whole new foreign-policy agenda, and Europe is given the opportunity to catch its breath after the destruction of war. When the Soviet Union prevents the countries of Eastern Europe from receiving Marshall Aid, the crack between east and west widens into a chasm.

Only 12 weeks have passed since February 21, when Great Britain declared it would no longer support Greece and Italy, and as a result of a geopolitical domino effect the world is changed.

Sofia

While Secretary of State George C. Marshall is giving his speech, the anti-Communist leader Nikola Petkov is arrested in the Bulgarian Parliament. He is accused of spying, tortured, and sentenced to death by hanging.

Cairo

And on the same day, the leaders of the Arab League meet in Cairo: the Grand Mufti, and leaders from Syria, Transjordan, the Lebanon, Iraq, and Egypt. There are movements pulling in opposite directions in the conflict over Palestine. The Grand Mufti and leader of the Palestinian Arabs, Haj Amin al-Husseini, is violently opposed to the Jews. He is supported by Syria and Iraq, while Egypt and Transjordan show some willingness to compromise. Some parties draw a distinction between Jews and Zionists, while others do not. Discussions continue.

The main reason for their meeting is to discuss the new UN committee, the working group set up to resolve the problem of Palestine. How should they respond to it?

The Balfour Declaration, Churchill's White Paper, the Woodhead Commission, the 1939 White Paper, the Anglo–American Committee ... So many committees have already held inquiries and issued reports. So many drafts have already been presented, so many proposals put forward on how to draw borders; so little has been achieved. Not yet another one, says Haj Amin al-Husseini. His line wins the day.

On June 5, the Arab League decides not to cooperate with the UN's efforts to resolve the conflict over Palestine.

Berlin

For the past two months, people have hardly been able to get their hands on any food. There are days when the average German doesn't even manage the allotted daily ration of 1,550 calories. The people are thin, with swollen faces, knees, and ankles. Three Berliners can fit into two U-Bahn seats.

Nor do the children in Berlin's schools get any history lessons. Not because of the food shortage, but because history itself has to be approved by all four nations in the governing alliance — and they are at odds with one another. There is no consensus whatever.

First of all, the Russians come up with a textbook which stresses the material aspects of past times, how societal changes are driven by economic and social conditions. But that is not an acceptable interpretation of history in the eyes of the Americans, who put together a version of history that they believe takes a broader view.

At the same time, the French prepare their selection of key events from the past, illustrated with reproductions of works by Eugène Delacroix. However, the French version of history is judged to be chauvinistic by the other Allies, and is not approved by any of them.

The British are painstaking in their approach, producing two volumes that are so bursting with detail that the first book only gets as far as humankind's discovery of the pendulum.

But the Americans don't give up so easily. In cooperation with German history teachers, they produce a concise text comprising key dates and events.

That is the situation. No consensus. No history classes. No food.

If the past is an open question, the future is equally unclear. What direction will Germany take?

Many think Germany will be Westernized, for the simple reason that so many of its inhabitants are still Nazis, fanatically opposed to Communism. Others argue that Germany will turn to the east instead; the Soviet system will give the Germans, with their faith in authority, a sense of security. Anyway, the heyday of democracy as a system of government is past, so they say, so if the Germans want to retain power, it is the Soviet Union they should be turning to.

Between these ideas, there is another that is becoming increasingly influential, a bizarre idea that was both unthought and unthinkable just a year ago. But now it is being articulated as a possible alternative — two Germanies.

Many people think the idea absurd. Two German states, each with its own form of government; two German capitals; two German citizenships?

Turin

Love and fury. Twenty-eight-year-old Primo Levi is working on his text, alternating between one state of mind and the other, switching between two extremes that can also be seen as twins. He has been trying to get his book published since January; since January it has been rejected by no fewer than six publishers.

Now it is early summer in Turin. A normality of sorts. A silence of sorts. Who wants to look back, when remembering it all is painful, when what happened happened, and the acts of cruelty committed cannot be mitigated by talking about them? That seems to be the tacit consensus of the majority. Let it be, move on.

Primo Levi works, talks to his sister, socializes with friends, writes love poems to his Lucia, but cannot bring himself to give up. What really hurts is rejection by the prestigious publishing house Einaudi. Now he is revising his text, looking for new ways to disseminate his testimony, his book, and reflecting on the title. Suddenly he finds he has some extra cash, so he puts his bicycle away and buys a Lambretta. This new freedom is celebrated with a trip to France, where Primo Levi is reunited with his friend Jean Samuel.

Does he tell Jean it's written now, the description of their time as slaves in Auschwitz? No one wants to publish it, admittedly, but does he tell Jean about the chapter that arose out of their captivity and friendship? He does.

Jean, the "Pikolo" of the book, remembers, but in a different way; he can name the same details, but from a different viewpoint. He places most emphasis on their first encounter, in the midst of the fear of dying in an air raid; on how they open up by talking about their mothers. Jean's memory is not Primo's memory, but that doesn't matter. He listens, wordlessly.

The description of the two young men in the concentration camp in Poland is at the heart of the unpublished book. The center of pain. Is this a man? The question encompasses both the reduction of the victim to victimhood and the reduction of the perpetrator to his role as executioner.

Imagine the June day under a Polish sky. Imagine the violence; imagine the sudden respite from it. Primo and Pikolo are detailed to fetch soup for the rest of the work party, and they take a roundabout route so as to have a little more time, a little more air, a reminder that something called freedom exists, even if just for ten minutes. The earth smells of paint and tar; Primo Levi suddenly recalls the sandy beaches of his childhood and then come the words, the lines from Dante's *Divine Comedy*, scraps from his secondary education. He explains to the patient Pikolo who Dante is, what the *Comedy* is, how Hell is structured, and he is gripped by a sense of feverishness. It is as if he is hearing the words for the first time, in a crescendo of fragments of memory, and he is on the verge of being able to explain everything there is to explain about human nature, its history, and the capacity for good and evil.

"Here, listen Pikolo, open your ears and your mind, you have to understand, for my sake."

Why he recalls the song of Odysseus, of all things, he hardly knows himself. But at that moment, the poet Dante meets the death camp of Auschwitz: one of humanity's most sophisticated works of poetry and one of humanity's most calculated abominations converge in the young Primo Levi. He is an intersection, civilization a fugitive crossing its own tracks.

New York

If this is a man, what then is a man? The question is also being examined by Eleanor Roosevelt and her working group at Lake Success.

The ninth of June is a mild, warm, and cloudless day in Nassau County, New York. One of the members of the working group on human rights has had the inhuman task of collating existing wisdom, and now the last two centuries' ideas about human value and dignity are presented in a 400-page document. Eighteen delegates from 16 countries are tasked with distilling a few drops of truth from the thousands of ideas extracted from earlier traditions. The word shining star-like over their joint and future efforts, leading them on, is "universality."

The Confucian philosopher Mencius is quoted for his 2,000-year-old precept: people matter most. The state is of less consequence. The ruler is least important.

Hindu thinkers and their high-flown thoughts are cited: freedom from violence, from greed, from exploitation, from humiliation, early death and sickness, the absence of intolerance, fear and despair. Thoughts that seldom touch the ground.

Oslo

On June 10, the Nordic Insurance Congress decides to introduce a new rule on *force majeure* at the earliest opportunity. No compensation will be provided for damage caused by atomic bombs.

Jerusalem

The UN delegates who are to resolve the Palestine conflict check into the Kadimah House Hotel on June 14. The city resembles a military camp, with troops, barricades, and barbed wire everywhere. Now that the Committee is here, the British are determined not to tolerate either illegal Jewish immigration or anti-British terrorism on the part of the Irgun or the Stern Gang.

The politics around the UN Committee are intricate. The British manifest a degree of indifference to it that borders on hostility. The Arab states appear to stand united in adamant opposition. The Zionists are doing everything in their power to get their views across. The Americans strain to avoid open involvement; whatever decision the Committee may take, the United States does not wish to be accused of being responsible for it.

The Committee convenes on June 16. It is met with leaflets, pamphlets, and newspaper articles: a cold shoulder. The Grand Mufti and the Supreme Muslim Council send a telegram to the UN Secretary-General in which they announce officially that the Palestinians will not cooperate.

The declaration is printed in the newspapers, black as ink and just as unambiguous: Palestine belongs to the Arabs by self-evident natural right. No UN Committee is needed, merely recognition of that fact.

Just in case anyone might not have understood the message, a general strike is called. Places of work, cafés, cinemas, schools, buses, taxis, and trains — all are brought to a standstill. No individuals or groups are permitted to testify before the UN Committee. No Arab may write to the Committee or take part in its meetings, either the public ones or those held in camera.

The Supreme Muslim Council concludes its public announcement with a seventh and final point: all protests are to be conducted in a very respectful manner, and in accordance with Arab traditions and national dignity.

At half past one in the afternoon of this second day in Palestine, the chairman of the UN Committee, Emil Sandström, makes a radio broadcast. He emphasizes that the delegates have no preconceived opinions, nothing has been decided in advance, the participants have totally open minds, and he wants nothing more than to cooperate with the Palestinians' leaders. Anyone who wants to write to the Committee, testify before it, or contact it in any other way is welcome to do so.

The English-language broadcast can be heard throughout Palestine. But who is listening?

Paris

Simone de Beauvoir calls Nelson Algren her crocodile on account of his broad, toothy smile. She is his French frog.

On June 24, de Beauvoir leaves her French pastoral idyll outside Versailles to return to Paris. She spends her nights tipsy in fly-by-night clubs which she calls "caves," where intellectuals follow an unspoken but established routine: at 11 o'clock they go to a given door in a given street, where there is usually a café. At night, everyday reality gives way to something clandestine, almost illicit. Wooden doors, opened by mysterious women, conceal flights of stairs down to red-carpeted basement cafés with deep armchairs, jazz, a bar, a piano. The artists of Saint-Germain-des-Prés dance and get increasingly drunk. Many wear their political convictions as openly as an armband, the atmosphere often becomes strained, and toward three in the morning the Fascists start fighting the Communists, while their respective girlfriends yawn. Others throw up in the corner, or fall asleep on the floor. Once the Communists have gone, the Existentialists pick up the gauntlet.

Nelson Algren is disturbed by these descriptions of nightlife, of attractive young men and women, poets and actors, by the thought that she may be spending her nights with others. De Beauvoir is angered, but soothes him with love:

> Writing to you ... is like kissing you. It is something physical; I can feel my love for you in my fingers when I write; it is good to feel one's love with any living part

> of one's body, not only in one's head. Writing is not as pleasant as kissing; it is even a little dry, and lonely and sad, but it is better than nothing: I have no choice left.

Algren, for his part, is keen on poker and betting on horses. He drinks bourbon, and fills his books and short stories with the world he knows best: drunks, pimps, drug-addicts, prize-fighters, bent politicians, and thugs. He has yet to reach the most lauded stage of his writing career. A few years later he will write the novel *The Man with the Golden Arm*, followed by *A Walk on the Wild Side*. He will receive awards, see his novels filmed, and experience success.

He grew up in Chicago with a Swedish father who had converted to Judaism and a German-Jewish mother, and calls himself a Swedish Jew. Now Simone de Beauvoir is planning a trip to Sweden, accompanied by Jean-Paul Sartre, and asks if Nelson can tell her anything about his father's country? No, he knows scarcely anything either about Sweden, or about Judaism. Instead, he asks whether she wants to come back to the US, to him? Yes. When? Soon.

Each time she sees an airplane gradually dipping over Paris, she thinks of Nelson in Chicago. And even when there are no planes in sight she thinks of him.

Palestine

There are rumors abroad. It is said that the UN Committee has already decided to partition the territory, that its members have actually been in favor of the Zionists' proposals from the outset, that the Americans picked them for that very reason.

True? False? Naturally there are preconceived views within the Committee. Both the Indian and the Iranian delegate are assumed to support the Arab cause — which proves to be true. Two of the Latin American delegates are openly favorable to a Jewish state: the Uruguayan because he believes in the Zionist idea, the Guatemalan because he wants to cause as much damage as possible to the British.

The Peruvian delegate seems not to have any predetermined opinions, but in time he will distance himself increasingly from his government's support for a Jewish state. The Yugoslav delegate opposes partition as a matter of principle; any other view could encourage widening divisions back home in the Yugoslav state, which is constantly threatened by various groups' demands for independence.

The Czechoslovakian delegate is close to his foreign minister, a man who wholeheartedly supports the idea of a Jewish state. However, the delegate himself proves to harbor doubts. Other countries represented on the Committee — Australia, Canada, Sweden, and the Netherlands — are generally considered pro-British, but where this particular issue is concerned they seem to show understanding of both Zionist and Arab interests. None of them are welcome in Palestine.

Emil Sandström, the Committee's Swedish chairman, is concerned at the Arabs' boycott. He holds a press conference, but no Palestinian journalists attend. He convenes open meetings, but no one from the Palestinian population takes part.

Behind the scenes, Sandström tries to contact the Grand Mufti, who will not meet or enter into any discussion. He refuses even to pick up the phone.

The Committee wants to travel around, see things with their own eyes, meet people on the ground. They begin with two mosques, four synagogues, a church, and the headquarters of the Supreme Muslim Council in Jerusalem. Then they travel to Haifa to visit a Jewish soap manufacturer, an Arab cigarette factory, a Jewish textile factory, and an Arab oil refinery, plus Mount Carmel.

There are also Arab–Jewish cooperatives run on a communal basis, but when the Committee visits them, the Arab employees stay away. Boycott. Neither journalists nor the Jewish drivers are allowed over the threshold of the Karaman Dick cigarette factory. All fact-finding visits to Arab organizations are subject to the condition that Jews are barred from entering. And that is how things continue for the UN Committee tasked with resolving the Palestine conflict: deep disappointment verging on humiliation.

On June 21, in the schools of Be'er Sheva, neither the teachers nor the pupils take any notice of them when they enter the classrooms, but continue their classes as though there were no one there. In the village of Rami, in Galilee, the residents have disappeared, and all that is left is a group of kids yelling abuse. The mayor who had promised to meet them cancels the meeting at short notice, and soon the delegates are obliged to take their own sandwiches, as the lunches that are promised never materialize.

The Grand Mufti makes it known that anyone who fails to obey will be risking his or her life. Not everyone agrees. Many within the Arab League consider the boycott to be a mistake that will cost the Palestinian cause dearly. But no one stands in his way.

During these cloudless June days, the Committee continues its round of visits in Arab Palestine. The members walk about in white shirts and straw hats, staying in the shade when there is shade to be found. They visit hospitals, schools, and businesses. Education, farming, and healthcare give the impression of being of a low standard and poorly managed. The delegation's overall conclusion is that the notion of an independent Palestinian state "is disconnected from reality."

Exactly the same form of words will recur after the delegates' journey around the Jewish areas, although for different reasons. These areas have sound infrastructure, roads, and water conduits, trained workers, and an incomprehensible optimism. In time, Arabs and Jews will live in peace together, the Zionists repeat, in time, just wait, it will happen. Their visitors, the UN delegates, turn to one another and murmur again: "Disconnected from reality."

The group moving in convoy along the roads of Palestine this summer is not a hopeful one. The beetle-black vehicles gleam on the desert road which gradually winds its way up into the hills and down again. Black as insects in the heat.

"The racial animosity is too strong," notes the Australian, summarizing: "[T]he situation is dangerous and insolvable [*sic*]."

New York

Charlie "Bird" Parker and John Birks "Dizzy" Gillespie have hit the big time: they tour Europe, play Carnegie Hall, the works. Thelonious Monk lives on a shoestring and gets no credit for his compositions. He hears his tunes on the radio, sure thing. Both "Mean to Me" and "Bean and the Boys" are hot items — but performed by Coleman Hawkins. Monk's songs, but no kudos for Monk. No income. The others, he would say later, hang out with him, copy his harmonies, come along with their sheet music and ask his advice, while he doesn't even get any recordings.

"Sometimes I couldn't even enter Birdland. Do you realize what it's like to a musician to hear his own compositions and not to be able to get inside [a club]?"

There's a new time now, born of the brutality of war and overshadowed by a menacing peace. Music is dissonant, rhythmic, and atonal. Countless Manhattan clubs open and close at an ever-increasing rate; Monk's melodies float out through the smoky night. But he himself makes his living as a pianist in others' bands, or by teaching. One of his pupils is the 17-year-old tenor saxophonist Theodore Rollins, known as "Sonny," who comes to Monk's home to practice after school every day.

Bill Gottlieb, a journalist at the jazz magazine *Down Beat*, notices that both Bird and Dizzy speak of Thelonious Monk as an inspiration and a model in interview after interview, and his curiosity is piqued. He rakes New York to find the man the greats regard as greater than themselves, the man he'll soon be calling the George Washington of bebop.

London

The term "black propaganda" flies like a raven from one British civil servant to another. The Foreign Office considers an anonymous campaign to calm refugees who have their sights set on Palestine, but abandons the idea before it has even taken shape. It won't help. Nothing will help. How could anything help when all the refugees want is to leave Europe, the murder scene, and go to the United States — or possibly Great Britain — though neither the US nor Britain intends to let them in?

The British Foreign Secretary, Ernest Bevin, thinks it an indisputable fact that the Zionists are acting as refugee smugglers in order to influence the sensitive situation in Palestine. The situation is serious. All attempts by Jews to enter the country illegally must be prevented. He therefore writes a personal letter to the foreign ministers of several European countries, requesting their assistance.

The Danish government replies promptly, reporting that they have already prevented two suspicious vessels from leaving the country. An exemplary action, and proof of their absolute loyalty to friends, exclaim the British, who immediately disseminate reports of the Danes' extraordinary efforts to Paris, Brussels, The Hague, Stockholm, Athens, Lisbon, Rome, Belgrade, and Bucharest.

In Sweden, British diplomats meet civil servants from the Swedish government. Gösta Engzell, a director-general and head of legal affairs at the Swedish Ministry of Foreign Affairs, says "he rather fears" that many Jews in the British zone of Germany are waiting for the first opportunity to travel to Sweden. Even though Sweden has the legal right to refuse them entry, Engzell says, the people of Sweden would react so strongly that it would be impossible to return them to Germany. Could the British authorities in Germany possibly see their way to preventing the Jews from reaching the Swedish border?

Buenos Aires

Der Weg is founded. The editorial office is at 156, Suipacha — an ordinary house in the well-to-do part of town, in the same street as the Swedish Embassy, though there is no notice on the door, no unnecessary attention seeking. Here, the first edition of a monthly magazine is created that will link the Nazis of Latin America with their counterparts in Europe. It will be distributed to at least 16,000 Germans and 2,500 subscribers in South Africa.

The editor-in-chief of the magazine is Eberhard Fritsch, a dyed-in-the-wool Nazi born in Argentina. Behind him stands Dürer Verlag, which publishes a long list of Nazi writers. The magazine's collaborators are equally at home in the Argentinian president's palace as on remote rabbit farms.

Adolf Eichmann, a wanted man, will enter the German colony's inner circle a few years later, when Eberhard Fritsch and his collaborator Willem Sassen want to write his memoirs. In order to collect material, they will tape many hours of conversation with Eichmann before a specially invited audience. But no memoirs are ever written. Eberhard Fritsch and Willem Sassen would like to see their ideology cleansed from accusations of mass murder and bestial behavior, but the talks with Eichmann are deeply disappointing. The project loses its shine and vision when Eichmann actually confirms the number of exterminated Jews — indeed, expresses regret that there were not more of them — and these tapes are later used as decisive proof at his trial. But all that lies ahead, in a future that has not yet become.

The Cascade Range

The whole thing will turn into a big flying misunderstanding. Not once does pilot Kenneth Arnold claim that they resemble saucers. He says they move like saucers skipping on water. But who flings saucers on water?

It's just after three in the afternoon of June 24. The mountaintops are covered in snow. A flash fills the sky. Nine vessels cross Kenneth Arnold's field of vision like a line of birds in formation: eight semicircular objects, with a crescent-shaped object in front. Let's be honest, there are no saucers that look like that.

Silence. Northward bound. Gone.

New York

Raphael Lemkin decides to abandon everything but his struggle to have genocide recognized as an international crime. His disillusionment after the first Nuremberg sentence, and the painful knowledge that his mother, his father, and many members of his family have been murdered converge, forming a single resolve: to constrain the evil of the world. For that, he needs the UN. So he leaves his job in Washington, gives up his $7,500 annual salary, and moves into a dingy rented room in 102nd Street, Manhattan.

Now that he has no regular work, he has no income either. Patched clothes, mended holes, and a constant struggle to pay for travel, correspondence, and rent — these are now his everyday reality. Soon he will be borrowing money from friends in Washington to pay his debts to his friends in New York. Though ashamed, he has no choice. Soon he will have fewer friends.

The UN is still new and unfamiliar with itself; it has yet to tie itself up in formalities and regulations. Lemkin finds a way into the system, even though he doesn't represent a nation. If only he can persuade one country to support a UN resolution recognizing genocide as an international crime, others can follow suit. All on his own, he tries to persuade everyone he meets who might conceivably be able to exercise some influence on the matter.

Among UN delegates, there is a feeling of guilt — he senses it, seizes it, and makes it his currency. He can exchange it for support and signatures, and he makes as much use of it as possible, all for the good of humanity.

Panama and Cuba are the first countries to back the proposal. Next, Lemkin manages to gain the support of the Indian delegation. After that, he turns his attention to the journalists. Every day. He buttonholes them in the UN pressroom, gives them angles, information, detailed examples of genocide. There is still no international agreement the world has to submit to — it is still possible to be sentenced for the murder of a single human being, yet to remain unpunished for annihilating a whole group. Soon, journalists make themselves scarce whenever he's sighted in the corridors, with the shabby briefcase in which he keeps his sandwiches, together with his newspaper cuttings. Gray-haired, in a double-breasted suit and worn-out but polished shoes.

Raphael Lemkin, the unofficial lobbyist. Always alone, always ready to steer any conversation toward the subject of genocide. He's no fool; he realizes that his single-mindedness disrupts the established order. In the end, he introduces himself with the words: "Here's that pest, that Lemkin." It doesn't matter. Nothing other than trying to stem the world's evil is of any consequence.

Women's organizations working for peace are particularly supportive in his struggle to have the crime recognized in a convention. They lobby their countries' UN delegates, and soon Lemkin collects a number of signatures. In May, the UN Secretary-General, Trygve Lie, invited Raphael Lemkin to draft a convention on genocide together with two other lawyers. Now, on June 26, it's complete. The document is submitted to the UN. Breakthrough is one word. Despair, loneliness, and poverty are others equally applicable.

Oregon

News of the unidentified flying objects gets around. Already, over a thousand people have publicly confirmed what Kenneth Arnold, the pilot, observed. The most ordinary of all ordinary things — the word "saucer" itself — has suddenly taken on an otherworldly, scary, and alien sound.

When Arnold enters a café in Oregon, a screaming woman points him out as the man who sees extraterrestrials. She's in tears. How is she to protect her children now?

He is worried and talks in confidence to yet another reporter. Maybe the whole thing has got out of hand.

Paris

On June 28, Simone de Beauvoir starts working on *The Second Sex*.

Munich

June can be warm to the touch, but these days are lined with steel. Cold war has broken out, and the Americans desperately need anti-Communists to combat the enemy.

Nikolaus "Klaus" Barbie — alias Klaus Altmann, Klaus Becker, Heinz Becker, Klaus Behrens, Heinz Behrens, Klaus Spier, Ernst Holzer — no longer wants to cooperate with the British intelligence service. Instead, he transfers to the 66th intelligence brigade of the US Counter-Intelligence Corps. His SS tattoo burned off like a repressed memory.

The Butcher of Lyon. Guilty of rape, torture, murder, and deportation; instigator of slow death and great pain. Responsible for deporting 7,500 people to the camps; responsible for executing a further 4,000 people; responsible for personally torturing Jean Moulin, the Resistance leader, until he died a protracted, violent death in 1943; guilty of the murder of 44 orphaned children and their teachers from Izieu, France, in Auschwitz.

The CIC pays well and provides protection against the French authorities, which want to bring him to trial. In a few years' time, Barbie will benefit from American assistance to settle in Bolivia, where his expertise in killing and torture will come in handy in the service of several military dictatorships.

Shurovo

Monday, June 30. Mikhail is in the northwest of the Soviet Union, where he is watching the invention of his life being soaked in mud, held under water, and buried in sand. He is nervous. For the past six years, he has been fully occupied with constructing, improving, and adjusting — and after the meeting with General Zhukov, he has a better understanding of the significance of all these efforts: the fight against Fascism.

The myth surrounding Mikhail is straightforward in a Soviet style of beauty. An ordinary boy becomes a soldier in the Great Patriotic War and is wounded. Without any technical training, but endowed with a miraculous gift, he dedicates his life to the service of his people and the Motherland. No mention of the fact that he and his family were deported to Siberia when he was 11 years old, during Stalin's Great Purge of his people. No mention of privation, stigmatization, starvation.

In the hospital where he was being treated for his war wounds, he heard his injured comrades saying their weapons were wretchedly poor, that there were too few of them, and that they even had to share. How could a war be won like that? And he also met a lieutenant who explained to him the meaning of the Greek word *avtómatos*, automatic.

DAYS AND DEATH

György Fenyö. My father's father. His surname translates as "fir tree." That was what he was called. What was his name? That depends on who named him.

It may have been Emperor Joseph II, though the two were born two centuries apart. My forebears lived under the Austro-Hungarian monarchy, and they were Jews. Thus they were obliged to comply with a new law introduced on January 1, 1788, which determined what they were to be called. There were 120 permissible first names for men, but only 37 for women.

Up until 1788, each father had passed on his first name as a surname, in an interlocking shifting cycle whereby each new generation bore traces of the one before. Sometimes people took their name from their place of birth. But all that was forbidden under the new law. Jews' surnames were to be Germanized and to remain unchanged from then on.

Many of the Emperor's officials enjoyed themselves thoroughly at the time, and plenty earned extra income when the new names were registered. People who were lucky or able to pay were given a grand name, suggesting gold, silver, rubies, or diamonds, metal-shimmering or diamond-glowing. If the official in charge had had a bad night or was short on imagination, the Jew was obliged to take whatever was on offer. Colors. Anything visible outside the window. Green, black, white, stone, fir tree, forest. If the official was a nasty piece of work, the name would reflect his character: *Saumagen*, *Wanzenknicker*, *Küssemich*. Maybe my forefathers were bakers? Maybe they were poor and longed to be blessed with white bread? Maybe the official was allotting classes of names associated with farming on the day in question? They were given the name Weitzner. Wheat growers. Fine.

But the Austro-Hungarian monarchy revolved restlessly around itself and its domestic struggle for power. Just 50 years later, the Hungarian component found a way of expanding its influence by registering more Hungarian citizens within the monarchy's borders — as if the kingdom were a ship and power would shift from one side to another, depending solely on the weight of the passengers.

The change that got under way in the mid-nineteenth century went by the name of "Magyarization." Jews with German surnames were instructed to swap them for Hungarian ones. The times repeat themselves. Nationalism repeats itself. Bribes repeat themselves. Is the Hungarian official responsible for registering names in a good mood? What can he see outside the window? A pine, or maybe a fir tree? Fenyö.

Now this is our name.

If events take place on the same date, can one say they are separate? If events take place with an intervening gap of 200 years, can one describe them as contemporaneous?

When I think of my father's father, rain falls thick, a gray curtain. György Fenyö.

A deluge of days has passed since his death, impossible to count, as no one knows when it took place. Some time in January or February 1943, perhaps. Possibly near Batúryn in Ukraine, or in Bielgorod. Time and again my father dreams about his dad, dreams that he has survived, that he's coming back. A returning dream about a return. But he won't return. Instead, rain falls and I stand in it: sometimes it's as fine as mist, sometimes a downpour, but it is always so dense that the view is obscured.

I'd like to think there were a few years of happiness in György Fenyö's life. He met a 20-year-old girl in Budapest and immediately fell in love. That was in 1931.

The following year, Lilly and György married in the Great Synagogue in Dohány Street, though neither was religious. She was fine-boned, quick-witted, Sorbonne-educated. He was elegant, temperamental, and charming. Were any photographs taken? There were. White veil, black high-crowned hat, two smiles, each turned entirely to the other.

And then — did they give a party? What did they dine on at the wedding feast? I don't know. Everything has gone. Her well-to-do family was not pleased that she loved a poor, uneducated man, but she went her own way. For a year or so, they rented a fine old house in leafy Buda and drove a DKW cabriolet.

I know György Fenyö had a perfect memory for music; after hearing a tune, he could immediately play it on the piano with an appropriate harmonization. I know he played Mozart's

Sonata Facile in C Major. I know my father's mother, Lilly, liked him to play Isaac Albéniz's *Tango, Opus 165*. That is all.

The memories trickle down through the generations. Stalactites of absence.

Their son, my father, was born in June 1936. I imagine a further two bright years in György Fenyö's short life, until his employment in Budapest's tar and asphalt factory came to an end. A new law decreed that Jews could not own factories, so his uncle lost the company and he lost his job. After that, he tried to earn a living as a photographer. That didn't work. He went to Paris to find employment. That didn't work.

On the outbreak of war in September 1939, he managed, by the skin of his teeth, to travel from Paris to neutral Lisbon. He was offered a job in South America, but the residence permit was only for him — not his wife and son — so he turned the offer down. Instead, he returned to Budapest by boat, with a wooden box full of oranges. How many oranges, were they done up in tissue paper, did they smell of sun and fresh sweetness, did they glow in his arms?

He traveled home to his death.

For a few months in 1940 and then in 1941, he was ordered to carry out forced labor for the Hungarian Fascist army. But he came back once more to Budapest, to Lilly, his son, and his mother, Amalia Weitzner. In the autumn of 1942, he was summoned again for the third and last time.

I don't want to write this. I stand in falling rain, falling death, words that evoke death, and death that evokes my words. My father's fatherlessness; this is the sound of the rain:

Under Hungary's anti-Jewish laws, Jews were banned from enlisting in the regular army. Instead, special battalions were set up for political dissidents and the country's Jews.

My father was a six-year-old boy. On the morning when the third order to report for forced labor arrived, he found to his surprise that everyone in the family was up before him. His father, György Fenyö, was seated on the sofa, his head in his hands, his elbows resting on his knees. The boy asked if they could go on an outing to the Danube, to go swimming or rowing. The answer was no.

György Fenyö, who had just turned 35, was dispatched in November 1942 to an internment camp in Nagykáta, with a bag containing warm underwear, tinted glasses to protect against snow-blindness, and some food supplies. The muddy camp was surrounded by barbed wire. Fear dwelt in the huts, and it was justified. The interned men could be called prisoners; they could also be called slaves.

The camp commandant divided them up into battalions and instructed their respective group leaders to make sure they did not return alive, as they were enemies of the state. Most of the guards were members of the violently anti-Semitic Arrow Cross movement. They treated Jews with extraordinary cruelty and brutality.

Was he killed by hanging or by shooting? Was he forced to prepare the way for advancing Nazi troops on the Eastern Front by walking out into minefields so that he was blown to pieces? Did he have to crawl on all fours, holding a bowl between his teeth and barking like a dog? Did he fall ill, was he placed in a hut that was then set alight? Was he forced to climb a tree and jump from branch to branch, then shot when he fell? Was he hung up by his bound hands and beaten? Were buckets of cold water poured over him where he hung, so that he turned into a lump of ice and froze to death at minus 30 degrees?

On December 31, 1942, György Fenyö was still alive somewhere in Ukraine. He wrote a postcard to Lilly with the words "you were the better half of my life." It is not clear to me what those words actually mean. Then he went to his death, his absence as real as rain. Unrelenting.

Once there was a woman called Alice Hoffman, the mother of my father's mother.

There is a photograph from the 1910s that shows her in a high-necked white dress. A very young woman, photographed in profile. Her hair looks like mine. Her face reminds me of mine as it was in my twenties. She was born on April 29, like me.

Alice Hoffman from Budapest married Béla Wollak, and they had a daughter, Lilly. She was an only child who lost her mother at the age of four, when gentle Alice died of dysentery after drinking unpasteurized milk.

I wish I could talk to my grandmother, Lilly, about the early years of her life, which were hard and lonely. But once we held each other's hands and danced round and round to music, I recall. Other than that, I have little experience of having a family. There is nothing but names, rain falling over names, names falling through the generations. Alice, Lilly, and the boy who would become my father. He was given the same name as his father, although that was not customary and no one can explain why.

They lived together for several years — the boy; his mother, Lilly; his father, György; and his father's mother, Amalia — in an apartment with one bedroom, a sitting room, a hall, a kitchen, and a bathroom. There was a piano. An oil painting hung on the wall, a portrait of Alice Hoffman. Normality persisted under abnormal circumstances.

When the Germans occupied Hungary on March 19, 1944, the boy who was to become my father was eight years old and already fatherless. He had only just started school when he was forced to leave, being a Jew. Neither his mother nor his father was a believer, and it was not until he was five years old that he connected the word with himself. A stranger, walking past him as he was playing, called him a stinking Jew. The boy went to his mother and asked her what "Jew" meant. Lilly answered simply: "There are two kinds of people, good ones and bad ones. And that's the only thing that matters."

I want to tell the story of my grandmother Lilly. She did her best.

There were relatives in Kraków: Imre; his wife, Erzsébet; and their children, Ida and János. When Poland was occupied in 1939, they were threatened with deportation, but, if they could prove that they were Hungarians, they might be all right. Lilly sold her jewelry so she could afford bribes to obtain the necessary documents, and that bought some time for four people, perhaps the chance of being saved, for the time being, one day at a time — time would tell. A neighbor betrayed them to the Gestapo. Whether they were Hungarian or Polish was irrelevant; they were Jews, and the family was taken to the Polish village of Oświęcim, known to the Germans as Auschwitz. Imre, Erzsébet, and 15-year-old János were gassed the same day. Twenty-year-old Ida was selected for survival and slave labor, first in Auschwitz, subsequently in Bergen-Belsen. I find this information about them in the camp archive. Not everything was destroyed. There is no mention of the neighbor's name. Ida never uttered a word about her experiences.

There is no flowing way to write this, no gentle stream of words, no reconciliation to be found in a gripping narrative. The sentences are staccato. Everything breaks, is broken again and again, faced with barbed wire. A time without mercy. Three times Lilly saved her son's life, the son who would become my father. But I am rushing ahead.

The boy lived with his mother, Lilly, and his father's mother, Amalia. There were days that no one can account for any longer. That is how life is; the days vanish and cannot be remembered; they merely pass through the body, leaving a deposit of time. Then came the spring of 1944, and the stars on their clothes were yellow.

The Nazis had tired of the fact that Hungary was not doing anything about its Jews. The head of state, Miklós Horthy, seemed to want to avoid the issue. Despite all the laws against the Jews and the open hatred, it was as if he was not prepared to take the last, decisive step toward actual elimination. Moreover, he had had one of his right-hand men hold talks with the Allies about a separate peace — a betrayal that Hitler took personally. So Hitler invited Regent Horthy to Schloss Kleßheim, Austria, and while they were at table the Nazis set about Operation Margarethe — that is, they occupied Hungary.

Horthy was allowed to keep his post, on condition that he replaced his right-hand man and that he obeyed orders in future.

Then came Adolf Eichmann. Over the course of eight weeks, 424,000 Jews and 28,000 Roma were deported to their death. It was very efficient. A purpose-built railway line to Birkenau, purpose-built platforms, special commandos. There are photographs. An SS man stood on the platform with his camera. The photographs were put into an album. He hid it. Someone found it.

The death that spread through Hungary left voids. Unoccupied houses, apartments with clothes left hanging in the wardrobes, families with lingering tenderness in their empty embraces.

Lilly, the boy, and his grandmother Amalia were not allowed to stay in their apartment. At half-past-ten one evening in June, Arrow Cross troops arrived and threw them out. Lilly, the boy, and his grandmother had to take what they could in a suitcase or a rucksack, carry their bedclothes on their backs, and make their way on foot to another emptied house, the assembly point. It grew crowded, overfull, chaotic. My father, the boy, lay head to foot with his grandmother. It was a house for Jews. His memories are a child's memories.

After the summer, the delicately built, vivacious Lilly was forcibly recruited for cleaning and other rough manual labor at the Radetzky barracks, where the soldiers of the Arrow Cross movement were stationed. She was issued with a special card which entitled her to walk through the city, despite the star she wore. She was able to bring bits and pieces of leftovers home.

On October 15, 1944, the Arrow Cross movement wrested power from Horthy in a coup d'état. There were soldiers everywhere. Now Lilly saved my father's life for the first time.

The day after the coup, October 16, was a gray day. For some reason, Lilly, my father, and Amalia were to visit a Christian friend of Lilly's. Since they had to walk several miles across Budapest, although Jews were not allowed in the streets, Lilly removed the stars they wore over their hearts. But soon someone spotted them; they were pursued by a young man on a bicycle. An assistant at the bakery where they bought bread, he recognized them, yelled after them. He pedaled after them. Other Hungarians in the street reacted. Threats as oppressive as thunder.

On Batthyány Square, the market hall had been converted into barracks for the ordinary German soldiers in gray uniforms — not the deadly dangerous, black-uniformed SS — and one of the officers noticed the baker's assistant on his bicycle and the three people he was pursuing. He intervened, his rifle at the ready, telling Lilly, the boy, and Amalia they ought to be executed by firing squad for walking starless.

What Lilly said, how she said it, how she managed, was something the eight-year-old who was to become my father could not comprehend, and which he is therefore unable to render. Besides, he was unable to understand German at that time. He remembers the fear, not the words. He remembers how the German officer gave in and agreed to let them return, how he called out to the German soldiers on guard duty: "*Diese Juden passieren lassen.*"

And so, passing guard after guard, they went back the same way they came. From guard to guard, the words were called out. How the Hungarians in the streets stared.

How the young baker stood rooted to the spot. How no one could touch them, now those words were being called out over their heads, following them like a vigilant bird all the way back to the Jews' house. *Diese Juden passieren lassen.*

Every day, Lilly went to the Arrow Cross barracks to carry out her forced labor. It seems that she talked about right and wrong with more than one Jew-hater. She called that "discussing ideology," and believed she could influence them. A few days later she saved my father's life for the second time.

Lilly was in the barracks when she heard that something had happened. Who told her? She heard that everyone living in the Jews' house had been arrested and taken to an assembly point at the police station in Bimbó Street. She left her work. She made her way to the police station. She brought an Arrow Cross officer with her.

Why did he go with her, not the other way round?

My grandmother Lilly, the tenderness I feel. The affection of unanswered questions.

In the courtyard of the police station, the people were standing in rows. Children. Old people. Waiting for the death march. For hours they waited, standing in line in the courtyard. Lilly got there in time with the Arrow Cross officer. They got to the courtyard in time, they found the eight-year-old, the boy, and his grandmother Amalia. They managed to get them out of the line in time.

That was the second time.

A time without mercy, without words. The remaining Jews in Budapest were concentrated in an enclosed area around the Great Synagogue. Easier to catch, easier to control. Now the boy, Lilly, and Amalia were assigned to an apartment in that area by the Arrow Cross officer. Lilly had to return immediately to her work in the barracks and took the boy with her. His grandmother Amalia went to the apartment in the ghetto. Later that same evening, when Lilly had finished her work and arrived at the house with the boy, it was emptied. A company of Arrow Cross soldiers had taken all the old people and children, and now they were gone. Amalia Weitzner. My father remembers a very kindly, affectionate grandmother. She was 73.

Someone else had lived in the flat before them. There had been deportation after deportation, a series of abductions. Now Lilly and the boy were to live there. In the cupboard, they found glass jars of homemade jam.

When the Soviet Red Army attacked Budapest, the ghetto was sealed off. The eight-year-old boy who was to become my father lay seriously ill, suffering from dysentery, on a blanket on top of a sandbag, in a cellar.

He, Lilly, and a few others sought cover.

How long did they stay there? No one knows. German soldiers made their way in and stole all the clocks they could find before withdrawing.

January was cold. Smoky air in every intake of breath when they made a fire on the bare ground. Somewhere there was silence, somewhere there was the sound of war. Somewhere up there in the streets, the tanks were rolling past.

A wall separated them from the cellar of the neighboring house. I don't know what color it was or whether it was made of brick. The boy on the sandbag doesn't remember it, yet the wall must have been there, because it was suddenly smashed to pieces. The wall broke, and the Russians came through. There is nothing frightening in the fragment of memory my father hands down to me. He was the boy lying on the sandbag, weak with illness. The memory is 70 years old, but it exists, it is dated, a decisive moment in a series of uncertainties. The wall remained in his memory because it was shattered and Russian soldiers came in. Lilly and the boy were saved. January 18, 1945. They climbed up out of the cellar and left the ghetto.

Wrecked lorries, hanging cables, dead horses in the streets, dirt, debris, people in ragged clothing, iron beams laid bare by explosions. There were houses without facades, with rooms, floors, and ceilings cut in half; kitchens and bedrooms cut in half; scenery ripped open theatrically; lives torn apart. Everything was brown and gray. Now my father is deeply absorbed by the work of the artist Anselm Kiefer.

They found shelter with the Christian friend. To be able to buy rice and milk powder for the boy, Lilly sold blood. That was the third time she saved his life.

Days and death. Lilly worked as a waitress in a café, but she had lost her faith in a future in Budapest. She decided to emigrate to Palestine. While she was waiting for an immigration permit, she sent the boy to the Zionists, who took him to the camp for orphaned children in Strüth, Ansbach.

The flat where they had once lived together — the charming György, Lilly, the boy, and his grandmother Amalia — was bombed to pieces, the piano reduced to wires and splinters. All that remained was the large oil painting that still hung on a wall, the portrait of Lilly's mother, gentle Alice Hoffman.

My father's father. An alien expression, a blank space in my vocabulary. Reported missing. Old photographs, archived documents from UNRRA or the murderers — none of these can fill the emptiness.

> Taken for forced labor service to the Ukraine on
> November 28, 1942, and perished at Bielgorod
> in February 1943.

In my father's earliest memory of his father, they are holding each other's hand, with a handkerchief in between. The sun is hot. They are on an excursion to Lake Balaton during the holidays and are on their way up Mount Badacsony. The mountain path under their feet rattles with loose pebbles, but the handkerchief prevents their hands from sliding out of each other's grip.

A white handkerchief — I picture it; its whiteness becomes the core of the memory — almost translucent with moisture between their hands, like a layer of time, both a closeness and a warm distance that binds them together. If my father is four years old at the time, he has two years left to gather memories of his dad.

Both my father and his father are called György, but I don't know why. György is the Hungarian form of George.

The man who became my father's father grew up in Debrecen, the son of a tailor. But why did he break off his studies? Did he fail at school? There is no one who can answer. Having no school-leaving diploma was unheard of; failing your exams was a source of shame that could drive people to suicide. Perhaps that was why he wanted to leave the little town and his father's tailoring business? Or was he adventurous? Perhaps he had no choice? But György Fenyö was not allowed to leave home until he had taken his examination as a tailor. He must have a trade, his father, Sándor, decided.

After that, György traveled to Paris. It was 1924; he was 17 and spoke no French. Naturally, he went hungry. After a while, he returned to Hungary, now to the capital, Budapest, where one of his mother's brothers gave him a job in his tar and asphalt factory.

He played the banjo. The piano. He practiced the accordion. Became a manager at the asphalt factory. Backcombed his thick black hair till it gleamed. Took portrait after portrait with the camera facing him and the self-timer half-hidden in his hand. That is how I see him now, as he wants to see himself then. Thus our gazes meet through silver and light, in an encounter that is both real and illusory.

Sometimes he photographed himself together with Lilly and his son. The boy was both amused and embarrassed, but still part of the trinity that was soon to be divided, part of the inscrutable gravity they tried to hide behind their smiles. Together, in black and white, they all look into a future that never develops. It all took place in the past, when everything was a continuum, and the days went by as they were supposed to, in an orderly fashion. Before the violence.

Memories like tombstones erected over a body that is long gone. What else is there to do, other than to describe the world so it becomes visible? I, who have always had a father, take his fatherlessness upon me. I, who have always had a father who looks into the future, take his memories and look back. Take what he misses, and feel it.

On my first birthday, they say, my father gave me some Hungarian sausage for the first time, and apparently I enjoyed it, though that anecdote comes from his memory, not mine. But I do remember us walking along a path through a deciduous forest next to a lake. I am four years old. He is carrying me on his shoulders, and I am holding on to his hair.

A graveyard is an inverted city. People under the earth instead of above it, in the form of urns and ashes, not muscle mass and 98.6 degrees. The transformation from being to not being. Those who enter to visit the memory of the dead remain outsiders.

In Normandy, the graves of the American soldiers stand to attention in white, while those of the Germans are monuments of darkening stone. Silent cities, where those who no longer exist sing inaudible songs about non-life to the living.

And then there are other cemeteries, all over Europe, which bear witness to absence through an even more audible silence — in Prague, in Berlin, in Kraków. The dead lie beneath a layer of time and a layer of dilapidation, their names written in ivy.

I visit such a place to lay a stone on my grandmother Lilly's grave in Rákoskeresztúr, Budapest. Rows of gravestones stand exposed to the elements, crooked and shadowy. Abandoned because all those who would have visited them were murdered.

1947. 1974. Two dates, the same figures, separated by 27 years. Time is somewhere in the shadows.

In December 1974, my father writes me a letter. I will soon be ten years old. The envelope bears the phrase "To be handed over now" in his handwriting, which is hard to decipher. He puts the letter in a bank safe deposit box with his loan documents and deeds. In the event of his death, it is to be given to me, his only child. But he lives, and it is only very recently that I have read the letter.

It consists of 19 typewritten lines. Eighteen of them express a father's love. The last, the nineteenth, is a single sentence, an exhortation. It forms a link between the dates. He might equally well have written it to himself in 1947, when he was in Strüth, Ansbach, as to me in 1974 in Kungsholmen, Stockholm. One ten-year-old is connected to the other.

And although I was never given the letter as a child, I have always been aware of the exhortation. Here it is in letters stamped into the paper by his resolute hammering on the typewriter:

Never pity yourself.

I try to assemble the year 1947 into a splintered whole. This is lunacy, but time does not leave me alone.

JULY

Paris

On July 6, for the first time, Monsieur Maurice Bardèche holds a copy of his book. He has traveled in a Europe he defines as a slum, and written it in rage and loathing. In *Lettre à François Mauriac*, he attacks the French Resistance for what he views as contempt of the law. He defends the Vichy Regime and French collaboration with the Nazis, and criticizes *l'épuration légale*, the judicial purge of collaborators and sympathizers currently under way to cleanse today's France from yesterday's dirt. The world is an unlovely place in Maurice Bardèche's eyes.

The new book explodes in the market like a bomb, selling 80,000 copies. Maurice Bardèche calls himself a Fascist writer — but one day he will be more than that.

Roswell

Sheep rancher William "Mac" Brazel comes across some twisted debris in the New Mexico desert. He reports it to the local authorities, describing it as wreckage from a flying saucer. At least one radio station interrupts its scheduled program to issue a news bulletin.

Delhi

Sir Cyril Radcliffe, a lawyer and one of Dickie Mountbatten's old friends from Oxford days, arrives in India for the first time in his life. It is July 8, and it is hot. Reluctantly, he has accepted the task of drawing the country's new borders, for — according to the Lord Chancellor, who appointed him — Nehru and Jinnah will never reach agreement. In the Lord Chancellor's view, Radcliffe possesses two enviable characteristics that make him particularly well suited to the task: his brilliance as a lawyer, and his ignorance of India.

He is given five weeks, no more, no less. The work is divided up between two committees: one is responsible for drawing the border between India and West Pakistan, the other for dividing India from East Pakistan. Would it perhaps be advisable to involve someone from the UN, as Jinnah proposes? No, that would take too long. Are there any other committee members with experience of drawing borders? Does Radcliffe take on any advisers? Does he carry out any field research? No.

He flies over northern India once, and looks out of the window. He visits Lahore and Calcutta. Apart from that, he sits in his bungalow in Delhi, shut in among maps, large quantities of maps. Responsible for regions that are home to 88 million people.

Sète

The SS *President Warfield*, once an American pleasure steamer, has left Marseille and moored in another French port, Sète. Its crew is composed of young Jewish Americans. What they lack in seamanship, they more than make up for in knowledge of integral calculus, baseball, and philosophy. The vessel, originally designed for 400 passengers and calm waters, will soon sail into world history at a speed of 12 knots and with just over 4,500 people on board.

At dawn on July 9, the passengers arrive in Sète, by train or lorry, or on foot: 1,600 men, 1,282 women, and 1,672 children and adolescents, all with forged visas for Colombia. Former concentration camp inmates with knapsacks, wearing three or four layers of clothing to make it easier to carry their belongings. Numerous pregnant women, and the orphaned children from the camp at Strüth, near Ansbach.

Four-and-a-half thousand people. How is it possible for them all to arrive in Sète and board a ship without the French authorities intervening? Is it because Sète lies within the constituency of the French Transport Minister, a staunch advocate of Zionism? Or because many customs officers, harbor workers, and border-control officials are active in the Socialist Party?

Or is because of the Tour de France? Today is the day on which the eyes, hopes, and adoration of the French are focused on the cyclist René Vietto, the magnificent young man from the Midi who is in the lead and looks like a winner. The Tour — the men, the sweat, the struggle of the twelfth stage — hasn't been held for seven hard years, but today it runs by Sète like a wild machine with spokes glittering in the sun.

Meanwhile, the refugees board the ship. It takes six hours. The makeshift beds in what was once the *President Warfield*'s ballroom fill up rapidly. There is no way back now — just men, women, children, expectant mothers, and elderly people, and the thought of the Gaza shore where they are to land.

Then nothing happens. The ship waits for a pilot to guide her out of the harbor, but in vain. The British will not let the French allow the ship to leave, so the French will not let the pilot provide assistance. But with 4,554 people on board, enough water for just seven days at sea, and only 13 toilets, time itself becomes the pilot. On July 10, the ship departs without either assistance or authorization. Songs, prayers, children's cries and hopes drift over the sea, a mist of anticipation.

Paris

The life of young Maurice Bardèche took a new turn when he left the village of Dun-sur-Auron and the modest existence of a son of an umbrella-maker. A scholarship enabled him to go to the prestigious Lycée Louis-le-Grand in Paris. As a gauche, rustic 18-year-old, he felt lost in the metropolis. But shortly after his arrival, something happened which was to set the course of the rest of his life.

In one of the open passageways around the institute's courtyard, he ran into two young men of the same age standing on chairs and declaiming poetry by Baudelaire in unison. One of the pair was Robert Brasillach. He was tanned, with dark, almost black, hair, a round face, and spectacles, observed the young Bardèche, who was also struck by Brasillach's style of dress and good humor. To Bardèche's surprise, the attraction was mutual. They became so close that their schoolmates nicknamed them Brassilèche and Bardach.

Then Maurice Bardèche fell in love with Robert Brasillach's sister Suzanne, got engaged, married her, and took her on a honeymoon trip to Spain during the Civil War. Accompanied by Robert Brasillach.

It was a friendship that would come to mean everything. Bardèche and Brasillach worked and argued against democracy together. In 1935, they wrote a pioneering work on the history and aesthetics of film; they wrote about literature and about politics. In their eyes, France was being weakened by alcoholism, a lower birth rate, and a Jewish invasion. The solution was to be found in the concept of heroism, men with a powerful physique, a cult of fresh air and sport, and attacks on both Communism and bourgeois society.

Je suis partout was France's main Fascist newspaper, with a print run approaching 300,000. Robert Brasillach became its editor-in-chief. Defining himself as a "moderate anti-Semite," he called for Jews to be excluded from the social community and, later, "removed" from France altogether, "including 'the little ones.'" The publication supported Benito Mussolini, took a positive view of the Spanish Falangists, and welcomed the British Fascists, the Romanian Iron Guard, and the Belgian Fascists. From 1936, it sympathized with Hitler and Nazism. Brasillach praised Nazi Germany's "well-organized beauty," whereas the French Republic was likened to a "syphilitic prostitute, stinking of cheap scent and vaginal secretions."

During the war, Brasillach used his pen to betray and unmask Resistance members and urge that they be killed. For this, he was arraigned in 1945 and sentenced to death.

He was not alone. Some 170,000 French citizens were brought to trial after the end of the war, charged with being sympathizers or collaborating with the Nazis. Of these, 50,000 were punished by being stripped of their civil rights — a so-called national degradation — and about 800 were executed. In addition, tens of thousands were extrajudicially murdered by lynch mobs and through show trials. Nearly 10,000 women were punished by having their heads shaved and being subjected to public humiliation for alleged "horizontal collaboration."

Yet Robert Brasillach's death sentence caused outrage. Much of literary France protested, even Fascist-haters. François Mauriac, the author and champion of the Resistance, visited General de Gaulle with a plea for the sentence on his political opponent to be revoked — this was, after all, a question of freedom of expression — and de Gaulle granted his request. Mauriac also took the initiative of writing a petition calling for Brasillach to be pardoned. Its signatories included Paul Valéry, Paul Claudel, Colette, Albert Camus, and Jean Cocteau, while Simone de Beauvoir, Jean-Paul Sartre, Pablo Picasso, and André Gide refused.

For members of the Resistance, it was precisely Robert Brasillach's writings that made him a traitor; his death would symbolize the death of Fascism. Despite his earlier promise, de Gaulle gave in to their pressure, and the sentence was reinstated. Brasillach died by firing squad in February 1945. Maurice Bardèche collapsed in grief and bitterness.

It is only now, two years later, that he is returning to his old self and to the world, writing two books in protest against what he describes as the falseness of the times, of democracy, and the hypocrisy surrounding *l'épuration*, the purge, the false penalties for false crimes. Having nearly gone under, he is reborn in a new shape, as a political animal: "I am a Fascist writer."

As soon as his book on the Resistance and the war trials, *Lettre à François Mauriac*, is printed, he starts work on the next.

Maurice Bardèche is lost. His country is alien to him, and the way in which its history is being written is equally alien. Hatred has got a grip on justice and put it out of kilter; hatred has become the new goddess of the age. Everywhere, he feels, hatred of the losing side is in evidence. Not that he has any particular fondness for Germany or the Germans, he clarifies. It is not the German people he loves, not even National Socialism, but bravery, loyalty, and the fraternity of combat.

Nor does he know anything about these men, he writes, these generals and statesmen brought to trial and sentenced in Nuremberg — though he reads all 40 volumes of shorthand notes from the International Military Tribunal, the first major trial. He knows only that they are on the losing side. That is all that counts. Their army was that of a small European country, he writes, which fought the armies of the rest of the world — and lost. Should they now also be accused, punished, and executed for that reason?

Maurice Bardèche suffers with those he considers the victims of the war — the people of Germany — and that is why he now writes the book *Nuremberg ou la Terre promise*.

The courage and suffering of the German people deserves respect. So he says what no one else is saying, writes what no one else is writing: that the evidence of a genocide of the Jews is forged. Of course Jews died, but that was as a result of starvation and illness, not of murder. All the documents that mention a "Final Solution" in fact refer to moving the Jews out of Nazi Germany, nothing else. The fact is, he writes, that what has happened to the Jews is their own fault. They supported the peace of Versailles, and they supported the Soviet Union. The real war crimes were committed by the Allies when they bombed Dresden and other cities. The gas chambers, moreover, were used to disinfect the prisoners, nothing more.

"I am not taking up the defense of Germany. I am taking up the defense of the truth" he writes, formulating his creed and writing his bible. Revisionism is born, and Maurice Bardèche is its father.

London

The summer is as hot as the winter was cold. Simone de Beauvoir and Jean-Paul Sartre wander around in the British capital on July 15 , warm and hungry.

London leaves a somber impression. So many buildings bombed to pieces, such shabby clothes, so little food. As if there is still a war on. Everything is serious and poor, Simone notes in a letter to her beloved Nelson. On the other hand, the people are very brave. And an increasingly dense layer of green is spreading over the ruins. Wild flowers, purple, red, and yellow, are growing in the bombsites, strange, unexpected gardens emerging where once a house stood. In the parks, people lie in the grass, unashamedly kissing. Fortunately, there is no shortage of scotch and soda.

Bucharest

The leader of Romania's anti-Communist movement, Ion Diaconescu, is jailed. Sentenced to life imprisonment.

Palestine

The American Ralph Bunche is the UN representative on the Committee tasked with finding a solution to the Palestine question, the one who leads much of the work behind the scenes. Just a year later, he will be asked to accompany Folke Bernadotte on his mission to mediate the Palestine conflict. When Bernadotte is murdered by the Stern Gang under the leadership of Yitzhak Shamir, it is Ralph Bunche who takes over as peace mediator, for which he will be awarded the Nobel Peace Prize.

But now? His view of the situation? Of the Committee and its work?

Its members are unprepossessing, lacking in competence; it is one of the worst groups he has ever worked with. It includes people who are small-minded, vain, and, in many cases, either mean-spirited or dull-witted. It is hard to understand how such a mediocre collection of individuals could have been entrusted with tackling so grave a problem. On July 17, Bunche writes as follows in a private letter:

> It might be a good idea for all the Committee members to get blessed at all the holy places and to kiss all the holy rocks from which the various gods ascended from time to time, since the Committee is expected to work a miracle.

> In my view the Committee will need to combine the
> intervention of Christ, Mohamed and God Almighty
> to do the job.

There does not appear to be any miracle in sight. Instead, Ralph Bunche organizes the Committee's work. It is also Bunche who finally draws up the two proposals for a solution, which the Committee submits to the UN General Assembly.

International waters

No sooner are the 4,554 refugees on board the SS *President Warfield* out of Sète harbor than they have company. They are trailed by two British warships, one on either side of the ship. Megaphone warnings, threats. As soon as the refugee vessel reaches Palestinian waters, the British have the right to board her. Everyone knows; everyone is on tenterhooks.

On July 16, another three British warships arrive. No one sleeps on board the refugee ship. The barbed wire along the railings is reinforced. Tins of kosher corned beef and potatoes are taken out to use as ammunition. On July 17, the refugees raise the flag with the Star of David and rename the ship *Exodus 47*, in the name of memory, myth, and biblical invocations.

Warning: I must warn you that illegal passage of your passengers into Palestine will not be allowed; and your ship will be arrested if you try to do so ... Force will be used if our sailors are attacked. Your leaders and all sensible passengers must stop the hotheads from futile resistance.

Reply: On this boat, *Exodus*, are more than 4,000 people,

men, women, and children, whose only crime is that they were born Jews. We have nothing against your sailors and officers, but unfortunately they have been chosen to implement a policy to which we shall never acquiesce, for we shall never recognize a law forbidding Jews to enter their country. We are not interested in the shedding of blood, but you must understand that we shall not go to any concentration camp of our own free will, even if it happens to be a British one.

At night, just off the coast of Gaza, two destroyers with their lights off move into place on either side of *Exodus*, making it impossible to maneuver the ship. British soldiers leap aboard, the blessed tins of corned beef are thrown at them, and steam from the pipes arranged around the gunwale gushes out.

Quite a few shots are fired during the ensuing two-hour battle, before the British finally take control of the vessel, which is then sailed into Haifa. One hundred and forty-six people injured, three dead, splinters of wood, a wrecked ship.

The Jews catch a glimpse of Palestine before they are swiftly dusted with anti-lice spray to ward off typhus, loaded onto three British ships, and packed off back to France.

Do the British realize that everything will be turned against them, absolutely everything?

Cairo

The art of death: *fann al-mawt*. The art of dying: *al-mawt fann*.

Introducing these concepts in earnest, Hasan al-Banna

turns the march of time toward our present, bringing the love of death into his version of Islam.

There lies the land, there the olive trees stand, and the rose bushes. Dust and bloom, dryness and shade. There, strangers force their way in and colonize, aliens trampling on the very soul of home. That is why, writes the clockmaker's son, it is the duty of a Muslim — indeed his greatest commitment — to engage in jihad.

An obligation which there is no evading.

Once upon a time, it all looked different. The Arab world, oppressed by French and British colonialism, dreamed of a revived empire. There, Jewish settlements in the region would help boost economic growth. The pan-Arabic ideas of the time encompassed both Arabs and Jews. Britain's 1917 Balfour Declaration, which supported the idea of a Jewish national home in Palestine, was celebrated by the future Prime Minister of Egypt, Ziwar Pasha. A few years later, Ahmed Zaki, a former Egyptian cabinet minister, congratulated the growing Zionist movement with the words: "The victory of the Zionist idea is the turning point for the fulfillment of an ideal which is so dear to me, the revival of the Orient."

In Jerusalem, on April 1, 1925, the Egyptian Minister of the Interior, Ismail Sidqi, had no qualms about inaugurating the first Hebrew university on Mount Scopus.

As criticism of immigration into Palestine became increasingly widespread, the Egyptian press responded by writing about Zionists and Zionism, but avoided the word "Jews" so as to protect the country's indigenous Jewish population from hate. Local Nazis in Cairo wrote to Berlin in 1933 to complain that it was pointless wasting time and money on anti-Jewish pamphlets, as no one was interested. Instead, they proposed, the propagandists should aim their efforts at the point where the interests of Arabs and Jews conflicted most — Palestine.

It might all have been different: if the First World War hadn't broken out; if Mussolini hadn't seized power in 1922; if Adolf Hitler hadn't written *Mein Kampf* in 1925; if al-Banna hadn't established the Muslim Brotherhood in 1928.

The Brotherhood's worthy social work — helping the poor and the elderly, and opening schools in disadvantaged parts of Egypt — attracts sympathy and garners support. But there is another side: the shirts, the marches, the idea of a healthy soul in a healthy body, the mistrust of democracy and the multi-party system, the dream of a revolution of purity. Echoes of Fascism, from one continent to another.

And so Palestine is to become "the market where we make a bargain by winning one of the two advantages, victory [over the Jews] or martyrdom."

Where *jihad* was once interpreted as "struggle," al-Banna adds death as its objective. Poems are written, songs intoned about liberation from the fear of death and burial under "an umbrageous shade."

Haifa

Two men are standing on the quayside at Haifa on July 18, watching the battered SS *Exodus* come in with her human cargo: the Swedish chairman of the Committee tasked with resolving the Palestine problem, and a member of his staff. They are wearing linen suits and hats to protect them against the heat. Were they brought here on purpose? Was it planned that the ship's arrival in Palestine would coincide with the UN Committee's visit?

The two men from the Committee watch the children, the first to disembark — over a thousand children — and speculate on whether this is a propaganda trick staged for the news cameras. The chairman, Emil Sandström, needs all the help he can get to understand Palestine and its undercurrents, both human and political. Here, too, he is seeking help, between the shadows and the flashlight whiteness of the day in the harbor of Haifa. Somehow, Sandström encounters the *Exodus*'s sole non-Jewish passenger, the Methodist minister John Stanley Grauel. "I have no solutions to the Palestine problem," says Grauel. Nonetheless, the Committee questions him, and it attaches great importance to his replies.

Mr. Rand (Canada): Did you visit the camps in Europe?

Mr. Grauel: When the *Exodus* was held back in Europe, I took the opportunity to travel to the camps.

Mr. Rand (Canada): How would you describe the attitude to Palestine among the Jews in the camps?

Mr. Grauel: Those I spoke to saw two alternatives — America or Palestine ... As I see it, these people have

> nothing to look back on apart from terror, and nothing to look forward to. They bear being in camps on Cyprus or other places because they know that in one to two years they will come to the land of Israel, and when two hundred people travel there, a further thousand are given new hope.
>
> Mr. Rand (Canada): Can you say whether there were any weapons on board?
>
> Mr. Grauel: In my judgment, these people had nothing to fight with other than potatoes and tinned food ... I would like to make a statement. After following the whole thing, I am certain they will insist on coming to Palestine and that nothing less than war and destruction will ever stop them.

The rammed ship being towed into harbor, the survivors who have nothing but the will to survive, the vessel renamed *Exodus*, which expands from a simple pleasure steamer into a symbol of refugee hope and refugee yearnings: it all creates a narrative disseminated worldwide, to every newspaper and to every newsreel in every cinema.

Once it is clear that the British intend to ship the former concentration camp prisoners back to France, the reaction is one of outrage and fierce criticism. Where the British seek to demonstrate steadfast adherence to principles and to deter any further unlawful attempts to reach Palestine, the world sees cruelty and a lack of common humanity. Returning passengers to Europe, to a France that is unable to provide for them, is inhuman, writes the *Washington Post.* Apparently the British temperament is such that the law must be obeyed at whatever cost, writes Léon Blum, the former Prime Minister of France. There is no scope for individual compassion.

Much of the world agrees. Send them to the camps on Cyprus, where other Jews are gathering to wait for a visa to Palestine, or at least send them to North Africa, people write. Do anything but return them to Europe. But the British carry out their plan. The four-and-a-half thousand Jews are shipped to Port-de-Bouc in the south of France and ordered to disembark. As if everything were complete, over and done with, the past reinstated. As if the voyage, the renaming of the ship, the potato battle, the hope, and the disillusionment had never occurred. But the refugees refuse to go ashore.

"Jews are in dangerous mood" British representatives telegraph to the Foreign Office. "Disembarkation by force is likely to entail serious fighting and there is danger of serious rioting on board." Nothing can be done.

Four-and-a-half thousand people seeking a life after death.
The heat. The wait. The world is watching.

Washington

Naturally, the news about the *Exodus* also reaches President Truman. It is 6 a.m. on July 21 when he takes a call from the Secretary of the Treasury, Henry Morgenthau Jr., who wants to discuss the refugees' situation. The discussion lasts ten minutes. Truman is obliged to take the issue up with Secretary of State Marshall.

"He'd no business, whatever to call me. The Jews have no sense of proportion nor do they have any judgment on world affairs," Truman writes later in a rapid, slapdash hand on loose sheets of paper which are inserted into the blue diary.

> The Jews, I find are very, very selfish. They care not how many Estonians, Latvians, Finns, Poles, Yugoslavs or Greeks get murdered or mistreated as D[isplaced] P[ersons] as long as the Jews get special treatment. Yet when they have power, physical, financial or political neither Hitler nor Stalin has anything on them for cruelty or mistreatment to the underdog. Put an underdog on top and it makes no difference whether his name is Russian, Jewish, Negro, Management, Labor, Mormon, Baptist he goes haywire.

London

On July 19, Simone de Beauvoir and Jean-Paul Sartre attend the premiere of two of Sartre's plays at a small theater in Hammersmith. After the performance, they dine on corned beef. Rita Hayworth is there, but de Beauvoir is not attracted — not even by the film star's beautiful breasts, she writes to her Nelson in Chicago.

It ought to be an amusing and interesting occasion, with both Sartre's brain and Hayworth's beauty, she continues, but Simone is bored. Jean-Paul is bored. Rita is bored. It is a very boring dinner.

New York

It takes a while for jazz journalist Bill Gottlieb to find Thelonious Monk in New York, so he claims. Inexplicable — why doesn't he simply stroll into Minton's Playhouse, go up to the piano, and say hello?

Naturally, he's seen him on stage: to begin with it was Monk's image that struck him most, rather than the pianist's innovative harmonies. The goatee, the beret, the glasses with gleaming gold sidepieces: Monk is a law unto himself, his melodies veering off unexpectedly, with pauses and hesitations in midflow. When the two finally meet, they hit it off, united in their great admiration for Lady Day. Gottlieb is also a photographer, with numerous pictures of Billie Holiday in his collection. He gives Monk a photo published a year or so earlier, which Monk tapes on the ceiling above his bed.

A type of jazz that is not dance music. A sophisticated, improv-based jazz that never seeks to ingratiate itself, nervy and cool at the same time. The very definition of bebop is also a word-portrait of Thelonious Monk himself.

Dizzy Gillespie and Charlie Parker speak of him as a god, but when Bill Gottlieb finally interviews him, Monk doesn't wish to claim the honor of being the inventor of bebop.

"For my part, I'll say that's just how I play."

There are many people contributing musical ideas. On the other hand, the piano may be more important to bebop than most people realize, he continues. It lays down the underlying harmonies and the rhythm.

He spends most nights at the piano, at Minton's Playhouse. Saxophonists, trumpeters, and singers come, do their thing, and go. Days and nights come, do their thing and go. Thelonious Monk carries on working. It's what he does.

Beirut

The unease among the members of the Arab League grows with each day that the UN Committee continues its work without their having the opportunity to put forward their view of matters. When Committee representatives contact them again, issue another invitation, and reiterate the plea that they call off their boycott, a three-day opening finally emerges. A meeting is arranged in the Lebanon.

The schedule is very tight, with conferences filling the days and dinners planned for the evenings, so the UN Committee's delegates will not have too much time to walk about and talk to just anyone. Yet a crack emerges; dialogue is within reach.

On July 21, the Arab League's delegation congregates in Beirut to prepare for the talks. A shared document is to be presented. They agree to agree. A few try to get the Grand Mufti to take part, to soften his stance somewhat, but he sticks a piece of paper to the chair that has been set out for him, and that states his views. He refuses to attend in person.

On the next day, they finally meet, the UN Committee and the Arab League.

The Lebanese Foreign Minister reads out the Arab League's joint position. It contains a demand for an immediate stop to all Jewish immigration into Palestine. A demand for the establishment of an independent Arab state on a democratic basis. A clarification of the fact that the Arab countries are linked with the Palestinian Arabs and therefore directly affected when the Zionists claim territories that belong to Transjordan, Syria, and the Lebanon. Finally, a declaration: the Arabs are convinced that a Jewish state will lead only to unrest and war throughout the Middle East.

There is an opening, too: with the creation of an Arab state, the Arabs would grant citizenship to the Jews who are entitled to it under existing laws.

The declaration ends with a clarification: "You cannot expect the Arabs to sit and watch this quietly without defending their natural interests." A Jewish state, if founded, "will not be able to exist for generations on end," because the "foreign element" will awaken the hatred of thousands of Arabs and they will use every "opportunity to get back what they have lost."

That is how the conference closes on the first day.

On the next day, the UN delegates have the opportunity to ask questions. The Arab League maintains its united front. The Czech delegate points out that they cannot demand 100 percent of everything; they must show some willingness to compromise. The Swedish chairman sets forth a variety of solutions for general debate: the creation of a binational state with limited Jewish immigration? A federal state comprising two independent units? The partition of Palestine and the creation of two independent states? All these questions meet with the same answer: an independent Arab state must be established on a democratic basis. Nothing else will do.

But outside the conference room, another message reaches Emil Sandström and his Committee. There are other voices, alongside the united voice; there is another tone, with some members of the Arab League able to envisage a partition. If Egypt assents to this solution, others will follow, the Committee hears. What matters is that no more Jews must arrive in the region. If the Arabs are given a guarantee of this, there will be a way to find a solution.

Confusion and frustration. Should the Committee trust the united front, the Arab League's shared voice, or the choir singing out of tune on the sidelines? On July 25, they leave the Lebanon without knowing for sure.

Jura

On the same day, the hens on the Isle of Jura have finally begun to lay eggs. George Orwell notes "Three eggs" in his diary. Satisfied.

Paris

Simone de Beauvoir writes to Nelson Algren in her rather childish but candid English about what she has been thinking ever since they met: is it right to give your heart to someone if you aren't prepared to give them your life? She loves him. Yes, she loves him, she repeats, but she knows she cannot leave behind her language, her country, her Saint-Germain-des-Prés with its cave-like clubs, not even for his sake, not even for the deep love she feels.

> When we shall meet again, we do not know what will happen, I just know that whatever happens I could never

> give everything to you, and I just feel bad about it. Oh, darling, it is the hell to be far away and unable to look at each other when you speak about such important things. Do you feel it is love to try to speak the truth yet, more than just saying "I love you"? Do you feel I want to deserve your love as much as I want your love? You must read this letter with a very loving heart, with my head on your shoulder.

Algren replies the same day. He has been thinking of proposing to her when they next meet, but now, after this letter, these thoughts, these questions, he has regained his senses. For both of them, a marriage would mean a break with their respective homes, from Chicago, from Paris — being uprooted — and wouldn't such a break be tantamount to spiritual and artistic suicide?

They agree to be together in a different way: she will visit him and he, if possible, will visit her, and they will then return to their homes and meet again later. They set their own rules for their transatlantic love, beyond convention and the law.

AUGUST

Frankfurt am Main

The world continues to fall apart. In a number of places, at the same time, ideas are taking shape of a third power, a unified Europe: the notion of dismantling national borders while nonetheless maintaining them.

That may be feasible. It must be feasible. There is no alternative. If nationalism was the explosive that ignited the First World War, skepticism of that nationalism now seems to offer a possible path to genuine peace. The word on everyone's lips is universalism. The nation-state has had its day. Europe must unite, or perish.

Here and there, first spontaneously, but soon in a coordinated fashion, associations and confederations come into being. Texts are published, political ideas are conceived, economic plans are forged. A United States of Europe?

A federation? Coordinated cooperation? The abolition of customs duties between countries? The fading away of borders? Including Britain? Not including Britain? The dream of a united Europe. No one can say exactly what will happen, who will do it, or how. No one knows when. But in the land that was once Germany, the dreams grow ever stronger and coalesce into a cohesive vision. When all the German associations that share the dream join together to form the *Europa-Bund* on the first day of August, they issue the following statement in a joint document:

> Europe can develop its spiritual life only if Europeans overcome the limitations and the egoism of the nation-state. It is up to all the peoples of Europe, particularly the Germans, to prepare for the development of Europe that lies ahead of us ... The economic problems, the communication problems that exist in all European states, the plans for a customs union, the idea of a shared European currency — everything points in the same direction.

Nothing has happened yet, the path has not yet been chosen, the decisions not yet formulated, adopted, or ratified, but it is only a question of days.

Manchester, Liverpool, Glasgow, London, Hull, Plymouth

On the same day the *Europa-Bund* is formed, August 1, the *Daily Express* publishes a photograph of the corpses of two British soldiers hanging in a eucalyptus tree.

The image escapes no one.

A few weeks previously, two sergeants, Clifford Martin and Mervyn Paice, were abducted in Palestine by the Irgun, a Jewish terrorist group. This was an act of revenge for the death penalties imposed on three Irgun members for violent actions against the British.

The Committee charged with resolving the Palestine question receives pleas from the families of the kidnapped soldiers, imploring it to act, to try to obtain their release, but it refrains from doing so: all this falls outside its remit. Mervyn Paice's father writes directly to Menachem Begin, the leader of the Irgun, pleading for his son's life, but Begin replies on the Irgun's radio station that all pleas for mercy must be addressed to those thirsting after blood and oil — the British Government. What is happening, he says, is the responsibility of the British, and their fault. When the three Jewish terrorists are hanged, the Irgun kills its two British prisoners and mines the land around the eucalyptus tree where their bodies have been strung up.

Can one disregard previous anti-Jewish attacks — such as those which took place in Limerick in 1904, when stone-throwing, assaults, hate propaganda, and a two-year boycott of Jews drove a number of families out of the town, and the anti-Semites were jubilant? Or the violent riots that broke out in 1911 in Tredegar, South Wales, when local miners took out their anger at high unemployment on the town's Jews? Or those nights in the summer of 1917, in the Jewish areas of Leeds, when young men came and smashed shop windows and threatened people? Isn't there a familiar pattern there, can't one even discern a British tradition of sorts?

The very same day that the first news of the sergeants' deaths reaches Britain, the Board of Deputies of British Jews issues a press release in which they strongly distance themselves from Jewish terrorism. Presumably they aim to ward off hatred, but their press release cuts little ice.

The violence starts in Liverpool, after slaughterhouse workers in Birkenhead refuse to prepare kosher meat until Jewish terror in Palestine ceases. Then there are attacks on Jewish individuals and Jewish property. In the first two days, nearly 200 incidents are reported in Merseyside.

In Glasgow, Jewish businesses are attacked; in Manchester, Jewish-owned shops and factories alike bear the brunt of violence. On the third day of the riots, up to a thousand people gather in Cheetham Hill, where they make threats, break up a Jewish wedding, and smash windows in eight Jewish-owned shops. Fires are started, police officers are sent out to guard Jewish homes. A number of policemen are injured.

A fake bomb is planted outside a Jewish tailor's in Devonport. Synagogues in Plymouth and London are daubed with graffiti, six of the windows of the Catford Hill synagogue in southeast London are smashed by people throwing stones, and the wooden synagogue in Liverpool is burned to the ground. Anti-Jewish incidents are reported from Hull, Brighton, and Leicester, in London, Plymouth, Birmingham, Bristol, Cardiff, Swansea, Devonport, and Newcastle. A Jewish solicitor is beaten up in Liverpool. Jewish shops in London are pillaged, and a large number of Jews receive death threats by telephone.

On the fourth day, a Jewish man is beaten up in Glasgow and groups of rioters go on the prowl in Manchester. Around 700 people gather at an anti-Jewish demonstration in Eccles and vandalize thousands of pounds' worth of property. On the fifth day, the plundering and destruction of Jewish property continues in Eccles and Liverpool. In Birmingham, a wall bears letters three feet high proclaiming: "Gentiles arise. Resist Jewish enterprise."

In Liverpool, business owners put up placards saying "We are not Jews" to avoid pillage. Mosley's Fascists hold meetings and recruit members. Over a thousand people are arrested. One of them is William Lloyd, who incited a 300-strong crowd to violence with the words: "Let them have it. We don't want the swines [*sic*] here."

In Eccles, Sergeant Major John Regan is arrested for egging on a crowd of 600 by yelling the slogan: "Hitler was right. Exterminate every Jew — every man, woman, and child."

It is weeks before British Jews dare to go back to their usual way of life. In Collyhurst in inner-city Manchester, a Jewish family puts up a sign outside their shop. It states that everyone in the family took part in the British Army's North African campaign. They distance themselves from Jewish terrorism in Palestine, adding: "We are all Collyhurst born."

More signs go up. In Liverpool, a shop owner points out that he is related to a well-known Methodist minister. His shop is left untouched, while those around it are vandalized. Other shop owners give clear messages: "Hold your fire. These premises are British," and "Don't make another mistake, chums. This shop is 100 percent British owned, managed and staffed."

The wedge driven into the British public severs the links between "us" and "them" without the use of anesthetic. A Jewish shop owner puts up a sign where his window used to be, asking: "Is this the reward for my son who was killed fighting for his country?"

Copenhagen

Denmark is a quiet little country, where nothing happens and people have too little to do, writes Simone de Beauvoir from

Copenhagen on August 3. So the least little happening becomes a big event. The best thing about the Danish capital is the harbor with its liquor, dancing, bars, sailors, and drunken, quite beautiful girls.

Geneva

The UN Committee has a few more weeks left to resolve the Palestine conflict. Everything has to be clearly established by the end of August.

On August 6, they take up the simplest of this skein of non-simple threads: British rule in Palestine. That must end. Everyone agrees.

With that decided, the delegates go on to discuss the alternative to British rule, and now the discussion opens up to encompass possible and impossible solutions, alternating between those presented as dead certs and those that are contradictory. The word "autonomy" is used a good deal. But whose autonomy? How? The concept of self-determination also crops up, with the same question mark.

The Australian and the Czech talk about making the region a protectorate for a period of time, until the situation can be reassessed. The Dutch representative speaks of a transitional period. They are doubtful, they agonize, wanting to sit on the fence for a little longer. The Swedish and Canadian representatives, on the other hand, strongly advocate dividing Palestine into two states, though they part company as regards government. Emil Sandström, the chairman, really thinks there should be two separate nations, while Ivan Rand from Canada advocates two states that form an economic and social entity, but are governed by Jews, Arabs, and others outside the conflict area. They cannot make any further progress today. Have they got far enough, or not? Who knows.

The following day turns out to be tougher. They discuss what they call "the extreme solutions." Suddenly a consensus emerges among all the delegates: neither the Arabs nor the Zionists can have their most far-reaching demands met. Three alternatives remain, each involving painful compromises: a binational state; a federation of two independent entities; a partition.

Yet another man tries to get in touch with the Committee and its chairman in an attempt to find a way through the impasse and a reasonable solution as regards the Palestinians' uncertain fate: Musa Alami. Despite his position in the Supreme Muslim Council, Alami loathes the Grand Mufti and all he stands for.

But rumors of the secret meeting reach the Grand Mufti, who immediately launches a counteroffensive. He makes sure the Arab press claims that Alami secretly supports the plan to divide Palestine, that he is actually collaborating with the Zionists. Instead of entering into discussions with Sandström, Alami is obliged to return home to defend his honor. However, he writes a memorandum to make the Arab position clear not just to the UN Committee, but to the rest of the world: *The Future of Palestine*. It is later published by the Arab Office in London.

In Musa Alami's view, even if the Jewish immigrants cultivate the desert and build new infrastructure, the Arabs will not benefit. People will not become any less nationalistic or less politicized simply because of an improvement in their financial situation. It is naïve to think they might be prepared to give up their lands and rights for economic reasons.

He emphasizes that both the UN and the Zionists fail to understand the real reason for the Palestinian Arabs' resistance: their profound conviction that an injustice is being committed. After many years of British rule and oppression, they yearn for independence, and the thought of their country again being ruled by others is a source of great anguish. No economic benefits or progress can outweigh the depth and the strength of that shared emotion.

Musa Alami wants the British to take responsibility for the situation, and proposes a compromise solution designed to be acceptable to the other Arab states; this would enable him to displace the Grand Mufti from the latter's position of political power. But every precaution must be taken in disseminating his message that there are other possible solutions. All the critics of the Grand Mufti, Haj Amin al-Husseini, act with great caution, since open opposition may mean their death.

In fact, Musa Alami's efforts have absolutely no effect on the future of Palestine.

What do they look like, the ten men around the table at Geneva? The Canadian, Ivan Rand; Karel Lisický from Czechoslovakia; the Indian, Sir Abdur Rahman; Jorge García Granados from Guatemala; the Iranian, Nasrollah Entezam; the Dutchman,

Nicolaas Blom; Alberto Ulloa from Peru; Enrique Fabregat from Uruguay; Vladimir Simić from Yugoslavia; and the Swedish chairman, Emil Sandström. Are they cheerful, concerned, do they laugh? The eleventh man, John Hood from Australia, is traveling around Europe, visiting refugee camps. Do they harbor regrets about their mission, these men tasked with resolving the Palestine conflict? Barely four weeks remain until they are to propose a solution.

Only four delegates support the idea of a binational state. Even fewer think a federation is a good idea. Only the Swedish chairman considers a strong independent Jewish state to be preferable, despite his earlier belief in a federation.

The Peruvian delegate supports the idea of an independent state, but on condition that it is small, that there is a halt to any further Jewish immigration, and that there is no question of an Arab minority remaining within the Jewish state's borders. Overall, his conditions are so impossible for the Zionists to accept that even he has no faith in his own proposal.

Several delegates see major advantages in letting the UN or other outside parties govern the region together with the Arabs and the Zionists. Others think a federation would be best, enabling local problems to be resolved locally.

Perhaps Palestine should be placed under a UN mandate for a decade and Jewish immigration restricted, then the whole region could become a single independent country? That is the view of both the Indian and the Iranian delegate.

Before the Committee charged with resolving the Palestine conflict begins drawing up its proposal, it is, quite simply, unclear which path it will opt for. The Committee is surrounded by secretaries and assistants who observe the negotiations. Things have not yet crystalized, says one of them. Everything is fluid, says another. The discussions are going round in circles, a third summarizes.

The United States

According to the latest Gallup poll, nine out of every ten Americans have heard of flying saucers. Just half have heard of the Marshall Plan.

Shurovo

On August 12, Mikhail follows the last tests with keen attention. Now only he and two other designers are still competing in Stalin's contest. Their inventions are dashed onto concrete floors, plunged into marshes, and buried in fine sand, filling every crevice, aperture, and orifice with dirt.

His weapon fails the test, but then the others do too. It is highly unlikely he realizes that his invention will one day make him a household name worldwide.

Germany

The members of the UN Special Committee on Palestine go their separate ways for a short while. Some are in Geneva discussing solutions, while, on August 8, others travel to Germany. They visit 175 Jewish children, the majority from Poland, in the convent at Indersdorf. There are 5,000 Jewish refugees, the majority from Poland, living in Landsberg. There are 5,500 Jewish refugees, the majority from Poland, in Bad Reichenhall.

And so on to Austria. The Rothschild Hospital houses 4,000 Jewish refugees from Romania. A neighboring school provides accommodation for 2,250 Jewish refugees from Romania.

Then they visit Berlin. The Düppel Center houses 3,400 Jewish refugees, most of them from Poland.

Hohne Camp, near Bergen-Belsen, houses 9,000 Jewish refugees, the majority from Poland.

The delegates seize the opportunity to ask a hundred of these deracinated, dispossessed, and displaced people a few questions. A kind of survey. No one wants to go back to where they came from.

If only the United States would ...? If Great Britain would perhaps ...? But when neither great power is prepared to admit Jewish refugees, only one answer remains.

> Question: How did you become a refugee?
>
> Answer: I was in the ghetto in Warsaw from 1941 until July 1944; then sent to Dachau where I was liberated and sent to the assembly center in Landsberg.
>
> Question: Would you like to return to Poland?
>
> Answer: No. My father, brothers, and sisters were all killed there; also anti-Semitism is increasing and pogroms will become more frequent.

Question: Would you like to emigrate to another country?

Answer: Yes, but only to my own country, Palestine.

Question: Why?

Answer: When I was in the concentration camp, I understood that my only future would be in my own country, Palestine, and that was why I wanted to survive — otherwise my life has no sense. I would rather die if I cannot go to Palestine.

Question: Did you apply for immigration into Palestine before the war?

Answer: No.

Question: Did you consider Palestine as your own country before the war?

Answer: I always believed that I would live where I could live well and in freedom but in the last few years I realized that that will not be possible in any other country except Palestine.

The Committee's representatives are dumbfounded at the wretched, dirty, and cramped conditions in which nearly 10,000 refugees are living in Vienna. The authorities will not allow any more in, but nor are they taking any responsibility for enabling the refugees to go anywhere else. Impossible, inhuman, acute. As if the war were still on, two years after its end.

After a week among these refugees from genocide, the delegates return. The expression they use when reporting to Sandström and the others is "cul-de-sac." No way out.

A three-page document now arrives from the Lebanese official responsible for contacts between the Arab League and the UN Special Committee on Palestine. He has visited the Grand Mufti, begging him for some hope of change, but the Grand Mufti remains adamant. So the liaison officer sits down and commits the result of his efforts to paper in a handwritten text. This document becomes the last attempt from the Arabs' side to counter the Zionists' demand for their own state, and puts forth their three strongest arguments:

- A partition would be in complete violation of the Palestinian Arabs' right to self-determination — indeed, of all their democratic rights.
- A binational state or a federation comprising two units would be utterly contrary to the will of the people.
- The Palestinian Arabs cannot be held responsible for the genocide perpetrated by Hitler, so why should they pay the price for it?

The document concludes with a prophecy: if any of the above should come to pass, there is every reason to fear that the reaction will be terrible.

The liaison officer confides in one of the UN delegates: he is depressed at his inability to influence the Committee. If no one wrests power from the Grand Mufti and changes the Arab position, the Palestinian cause will be lost.

Karachi and Delhi

Midnight. Now it is happening. Pakistan and India become two separate, independent nations. More than ten million people are forced to uproot themselves: the Muslims travel to one part of the subcontinent, the Hindus to another.

If "now" actually existed, that is. In Pakistan, the time reaches midnight 30 minutes before the time in India. Even though everything happens at the same time, the two new nations celebrate their independence on different dates.

Los Angeles

"I am aware of the fact that it will take several decades before one can expect there to be any understanding of my work," observes the composer Arnold Schoenberg. "The perceptions of both musicians and listeners must mature first."

The world has reached the nuclear age, whose soundtrack is dissonance, charged with ideology. To the Americans, Schoenberg's music is Bolshevism; they accuse every note of being autarkic and of equal value.

Arnold Schoenberg now combines his method of composition — according to which no harmonies or chords may take precedence over others, in which the new age is to be made audible — with the tales he has heard of the Jewish uprising in Warsaw. Bringing together resistance, humiliation, and death, he composes *A Survivor from Warsaw* for a narrator, choir, and orchestra. Six minutes long, with an English libretto, the work is written over 11 days in August. Schoenberg's instructions specify that the German text in the libretto is to be spoken with a Prussian accent, forming a built-in accusation.

The gas chambers find their way into classical music; violence is countered by prayer, death by rebellion, the oppressors by the oppressed. How the Jewish fighters were forced to take refuge in the sewers of Warsaw to elude their persecutors.

Geneva

Eleven men are seated around a table. A federation? Partition? Borders? Self-determination? A protectorate? Today, August 16, they again bring their deliberations on Palestine to a close without having reached any solution.

New York

The darkness within him flows out into the world's darkness. On a block of lined paper, again and again, Raphael Lemkin scrawls the words *Quo Vadis*: whither goest thou? In different writing, with different degrees of pressure, in different shades of black. Ten, fifteen, twenty versions: *Quo Vadis*. In between: "why?" He asks, but there is no response.

What is making Lemkin ill is this: the West allowed mass murder to take place, without a word of protest. That means the victims of murder are being murdered once again — and not them alone, but truth itself. Someone says he is insane. Yes, the world is making him insane. But that no longer matters. Nothing matters, not money, not honor, material goods, or a good life: all is turning to ashes, trash, trivia. Who can complain of illness, sleeplessness, nightmares, who can say the August heat in New York is unbearable, when there is no heat that compares with the furnaces of Dachau and Auschwitz? Since he cannot afford a doctor, he diagnoses himself: genociditis. Sick with genocide.

Stockholm

And the Swedes, writes Simone de Beauvoir on August 17, are the dullest of people. They are so dull that they yawn their way through their lives, and they are so bored that it amuses them to bore others.

In Stockholm, she buys a pair of red shoes.

Jura

Time is running out for George Orwell; maybe he suspects that himself. Yet no fear is conveyed by the pen with which he writes his diary. Not even in the bald account he gives of the incident on August 19, when the dinghy carrying Orwell, his three-year-old son, and two friends is caught up in the Corryvreckan Whirlpool. The outboard motor works loose and sinks to the bottom of the Atlantic; they row toward Eilean Mòr, an uninhabited island, but then the boat capsizes, with the three-year-old underneath. They manage to pull him out. Oars, picnic, cargo — everything is lost. The island that saves them is bare of wood, but they gather grass and get Orwell's lighter to work, so they can dry their clothes at the fire. Three hours later, some passing fishermen give them a lift home to the house on Jura. If thoughts of life's end frighten Orwell, that is not betrayed by his diary. "Were all nearly drowned," he writes. No more, no less.

Nuremberg

All over Europe, the trials are taking place at the same time — in Kraków, Nuremberg, Hamburg, Venice. The dimensions of the violence are measured and noted down. Lawyers, and an increasingly indifferent general public, gather around the black hole of morality and try to sense the bottom. This year, the following trials begin, continue, or are brought to a conclusion:

- The trial of Field Marshal Erhard Milch, charged with war crimes and crimes against humanity.
- The trial of 16 lawyers and judges responsible for the laws that facilitated murder on grounds of "racial hygiene."
- The trial of Oswald Pohl and other SS officers for actively participating in and organizing the so-called Final Solution.
- The trial of Friedrich Flick and others on grounds including the exploitation of slave laborers in their industries.
- The trial of the directors of IG Farben for exploiting slave laborers in their industries and manufacturing the lethal gas Zyklon B, among other reasons.
- The trial of 12 generals on grounds including the mass murder of civilians in Greece, Yugoslavia, and Albania.
- The trial of 14 officials responsible for the Nazi program of "racial purification" conducted through forced abortions,

the abduction of children, and the expulsion of population groups.
- The trial of the directors of the Krupp Group for exploiting slave laborers.
- The trial of 14 high-ranking military figures charged with crimes against peace, war crimes, and crimes against humanity.
- The trial of doctors and nurses from the Hadamar Institute, guilty of murdering thousands of people with physical and mental disabilities.
- The trial of the Auschwitz guards.
- The trial of Rudolf Höss, commandant of Auschwitz.
- The trial of the *Einsatzgruppen*.

On August 20, judgment is passed on the 23 doctors indicted for carrying out medical experiments on people in the camps. Several of them claim in their defense that their experiments are no different from similar experiments carried out by American doctors. They argue that there is no international law that draws a line between lawful and unlawful experiments on human beings.

Concerned at these assertions, two doctors associated with the prosecution define the conditions under which experiments can be conducted on human beings, to ensure they are in line with medical ethics. In their first point, they state that experiments on people must be voluntary. The research must have positive results for society, and any risks to people taking part in such experiments must be minimized. Their Nuremberg

Code becomes a component of the judgment, of future research ethics, and of the declaration on human rights that is in the process of being drawn up. The lack of morality is to be combated through morality.

Does the world become slightly better on this day?

Malmö

While Per Engdahl is spare and birdlike in build, his visions are palatial in scale. Excused military service because of poor eyesight, he substitutes words for weapons: assembling, deploying, whetting them. Whenever he speaks in public, his listeners are seized by a strange emotion — as though Engdahl were the center and all else peripheral — and he gathers them to him.

He has a dream which he will live for the next 20 years of his life. And that dream spreads, the network spreads, and Engdahl's renown spreads. The discussions on "nationalistic cooperation," pursued through correspondence, by telephone, and via colleagues dispatched abroad by Engdahl, grow more and more intense. Below-the-surface intense, beyond-monitoring intense, no-evidence-left-for-posterity intense.

The issues that currently preoccupy him will produce results. The first visible building block, the first event that will astound the world just three years from now, will be the great congress in Rome. In October 1950, leading Nazis and Fascists from Italy, Great Britain, Spain, Portugal, France, Switzerland, Austria, Germany, the Netherlands, Belgium, and Sweden will meet for a conference. The black flower will bloom.

While the democratically minded embrace the concept of universality, Fascism mutates from nationalism into an international nationalism. An idea that everyone will be absorbed into a single white body, with a single black heart.

In Italy, the MSI passes on Mussolini's ideas like an unquenchable torch. It is embedded in a network linked with Fascists and Nazis in Austria, Switzerland, Great Britain, France, Belgium, the Netherlands, Scandinavia, Spain, Latin America, and the Middle East.

A network surrounds the Swedish Fascist leader Per Engdahl, with another around his British opposite number, Oswald Mosley. Soon these networks will link up, in accordance with the plan for a resurrected third Europe, one they want to be neither capitalist nor communist: a fortress with an economy based on raw materials and manufactures from the African colonies, which will abandon democracy to its emasculated fate.

So: a conference to be held in Rome, from 22 to 25 October 1950. Before the journey, Engdahl learns Italian, which will earn him both results and prestige. And maybe he is anxious about being stopped or slandered, maybe his actions signal vanity or a longing for legitimacy — it isn't clear which — but he contacts a high-ranking civil servant in the US Department of Defense. In a letter, he stresses the anti-Communist aims of the Rome Congress. In response, he receives a letter wishing him every success, written on paper with the official Pentagon letterhead. In the Cold War power struggle, the enemy of one's enemy becomes a friend.

Oswald Mosley is there. There too is Karl-Heinz Priester, once part of the Hitler Youth leadership, who declares:

> While Russia seeks to convert Europe to Bolshevism, the West seeks to colonise us ... To resist the oppressors of Germany and Europe, the front generation extends its hands to all national forces in all countries, in order to cooperate and make Europe the world's third great power. To achieve that, the front generation in all the countries concerned will need to demolish obstacles such as provincial nationalism and alien democratic principles.

Per Engdahl will take over where Priester finishes, setting forth his plan for a structure and an administration that will make all this possible. Applause. A totally centralized Europe under a strong leader.

The Congress also resolves to make contact with the *Asociación Argentina Europa*, a committee led by Nazi Germany's most successful pilot, Hans-Ulrich Rudel. He is one of those now setting up Nazi escape routes in cooperation with the Vatican.

The 1950 Rome Congress will be a success for the far right, and sees Per Engdahl's coronation as the movement's Caesar. The ten points on Europe's future that he draws up, the *Carta di Roma*, are adopted as the official final document. The word "democracy" is left out.

The conference participants want to meet again soon. But preferably in a quieter place than Rome, somewhere where

Nazi occupation has not clouded the vision of an authoritarian future, a peripheral meeting place beyond the gaze of the world's anti-Nazis. The answer comes from Per Engdahl: Malmö.

One day, National Socialism will arise in a new shape and march again, says Engdahl. His Malmö Conference in May 1951 will be the first step. Participants from all over Europe are invited. Engdahl contacts Sweden's Prime Minister, Tage Erlander, and receives his personal guarantee that the foreign guests' visa applications will be fast-tracked.

But not everything will go according to plan. At the last moment, Oswald Mosley announces that he cannot attend, possibly because of the conflict flaring up between him and Karl-Heinz Priester.

In their visa applications, the German guests give private reasons for their trip to Malmö. One claims he is going to visit family, another is lecturing on radio technology, a third one wants to visit Sweden "to exchange ideas after engaging in correspondence." But the Swedish Aliens Commission receives secret information from the West German police about the guests' Nazi activities. One of the invitees, for instance, represents the Nazi magazine *Der Weg*. He and another six Germans are refused permission to enter Sweden. They include Karl-Heinz Priester and his wife.

Initially, Per Engdahl hopes that the terrifying Colonel Otto Skorzeny, temporarily resident in Madrid, will be able to take part. Skorzeny is best known for having rescued Mussolini from imprisonment at Hitler's personal behest. After the war, he was taken prisoner in Darmstadt, where several reports conclude that he is organizing networks to help Nazis flee the country. The network is initially known as the Brotherhood and later possibly as "Odessa," though no proof is ever provided. It is said that he is also building up a network of safe houses in Germany for the white fugitives, calling himself "*Die Spinne.*" But what is true, what is concealed, what is myth, and what are unbelievable facts is unclear. Inexplicably, Skorzeny escapes from captivity and makes his way to Spain.

The Swedish Security Service are very concerned that Engdahl is in contact with such a "dangerous" person. Now Skorzeny is added to the party guest list as the thirteenth fairy, and Per Engdahl writes specially to the Swedish authorities, asking them to accept the Colonel's visa application for the Malmö Congress.

But something gets in the way. Other Germans protest vigorously at Skorzeny's presence. Engdahl is obliged to undo everything he has done, ring the civil servant responsible at the Aliens Commission, and ask him to reject Skorzeny's visa application.

Incidentally, Prime Minister Tage Erlander is as good as his word when it comes to fast-tracking visa applications; it takes the civil servants just seven days to reject them.

Despite all this, some 60 European Nazis and Fascists meet in 1951 to confer and plan in Hotel Kramer on Malmö's Stortorget. This is the birth of the Europäische Soziale Bewegung, also known as the Malmö Movement. The network aims to build a new Europe free of alien elements, free of Communism, free of feminism, and free of democracy.

Malmö becomes the center of the movement, which is steered by a council comprising four men: the Italian Movimento Sociale Italiano leader and Fascist Augusto De Marsanich, German Nazi Karl-Heinz Priester, Monsieur Maurice Bardèche, and the Swede Per Engdahl as leader, the spider in the great spider's web, the correspondent in the network of correspondence, the ideologue who, together with his closest collaborators, spins his ideas around Europe as if it were his prey.

The draft declarations and proposals reveal their tone, dream, and ambition:

> After a thousand years of conflict between the peoples of Europe and a half-century of destructive war which has devastated the world economy and resulted in unutterable suffering, the peoples of the West and their culture have been brought to the brink of a precipice. To prevent a final downfall, there is a need to depart from the well-trodden paths of global politics, whereupon a new age of human progress will be ushered in.

A new world within reach. A "front generation" that is to create that world. Ten points which will lay the foundations, collected in a document which concludes with the words:

> The material standard depends upon the moral standard. Social and economic progress is impossible without moral progress. The renewal of Europe must also be a spiritual renewal of humanity, society, and the state.

The question of race must be dealt with. Is it even possible to use the word in Europe after ... well, you know? The Swiss Nazis have a clear position on this:

> By "culture," we mean that which is most sacred to us. Culture is a manifestation of race. It disappears if a race disappears. For that reason, our foremost objective — preserving our culture — implies preserving our race. Given that the peoples of Europe are racially related, a European culture exists. To preserve that European culture, we intend to create unity throughout the continent.

Per Engdahl and Maurice Bardèche are both poets, journalists, men of words. They know that languages contain values and principles. It is impossible to establish who thinks the thought first, where the influence comes from, but the shift begins, from one to the other. From race to culture.

Later on, Bardèche will observe that it is precisely the idea of replacing the notion of heredity by that of culture that makes everything so much easier for the extreme right. Hence it can "recognize and even ... assert the diversity of races," while at the same time "being able even to call itself anti-racist."

The German Fascists want to earmark funds to help Nazi prisoners of war. The Italian Fascists state that the constitution of the "State of Europe" will be an organic expression of the European soul, and stress the principle of Europe's undeniable cultural superiority in relation to the rest of the world.

Great days, great thoughts. A monthly magazine is founded by the former stormtrooper Herbert Böhme and the former SS man Arthur Ehrhardt, who served under Himmler. The five-man board of editors naturally includes Per Engdahl. And his life's work, a book entitled *Västerlandets förnyelse*, is adopted as the movement's ideological basis.

The ideas, the network spread rapidly. Around 40 movements from across Europe join. One of them is the Hungarist movement led by General Árpád Henney. His organization is regarded as the successor to Hungary's deeply anti-Semitic Arrow Cross movement. He also leads a military combat organization, and is on the editorial board of *Út és Cél*, a propaganda sheet banned in Austria on account of its violent anti-Semitic content and unalloyed Nazism. The editorial board then moves to West Germany.

All this lies within a few years' reach. The steps which Per Engdahl takes now, in 1947, the words that are spoken and those that are whispered, the plans that are adopted, all of them lead on into the shared Fascist future. And there is more to come.

Port-de-Bouc

This cannot go on any longer. The refugees on board the British ships in Port-de-Bouc cannot just stay there for one hot August week after the other. Someone calls the British military vessels floating concentration camps. Is there any possibility that Great Britain's loyal friend Denmark might consider taking in the refugees?

This request is sent discreetly to the Danish Government, which turns it down. Denmark is already overloaded with

250,000 German refugees from East Prussia and other eastern German regions who have fled before the Red Army.

There is only one solution left for Britain.

When rumors of what the British are planning to do reach the US State Department, the Americans urge them against it. Public opinion, they write to the British. Feelings. You can't really mean it? This could even affect relations between the United States and Britain, they write.

But the British stand by their decision. They cannot allow Jews to travel to Palestine illegally; there is an agreement in place with the Arabs which states that no more than 1,500 refugees can be admitted each month. Moreover, the British reason, they don't want to risk influencing the UN Special Committee on Palestine. But it will be their decision, above all, that will soon shift worldwide sympathies toward the Zionists.

On August 22, the message is conveyed to the *Exodus* refugees, and thereby to the world. The people on board three British vessels — more than 4,000 of them — are given 24 hours to disembark in France. If they do not, they will be returned to Germany.

The world is baffled. Germany? To the ashes of Europe, the very scene of the murder? Port-de-Bouc is full of journalists who spread the news while the world's condemnation grows in strength. Hitler's triumph, people call it when the democracies force the Jews back to Germany, the country from which they have only just been saved. The condemnation continues when the refugees are forced to disembark in Hamburg. Great Britain is criticized for brutality and inhumanity, and called cold, blind, and uncompromising.

Only the editorial writer at the *New York Times* directs his scrutiny at his own government and its policy, noting that if the United States had opened its borders after the war, these worn-out refugees would be American citizens and useful members of society by now. A waste, painful.

Geneva

The members of the UN Committee gather in Geneva to vote on the Palestine question. There is no clear way forward. Two alternatives have been formulated. One is a federation with two provinces, one Jewish and one Arab; immigration will be limited so that the Jewish population does not end up in the majority. The other is to create two independent states forming an economic union, a plan lacking any details about borders or Jerusalem. Schisms arise. The delegates waver between the alternatives. Their motives change.

In the morning, the Peruvian delegate says that since there are important details missing from the partition plan, he will support the proposal of a federation.

The Swedish, Canadian, Guatemalan, and Uruguayan delegates work up some enthusiasm for the two-state solution, but disagree on how the borders are to be drawn.

The Australian surprises everyone by saying they should stop now and hand everything over to the UN General Assembly. The Dutchman and the Czech gratefully seize the opportunity to avoid having to vote, while the chairman, Emil Sandström, refuses to accept a situation in which the Committee would fail to fulfill its purpose: putting forward a proposal for a solution. Deadlock, stasis, stalemate. They have three days left to come up with an answer to the world's question about Palestine.

But then the proponents of a federation propose that both the proposal for partition and the proposal for a federation be put before the UN General Assembly for discussion, regardless of how the Committee votes. That calms the atmosphere, and the men can go on to actually hold a vote.

The Peruvian announces that he has changed his mind and can vote for a partition of Palestine, provided that Jerusalem is placed under an international regime. The Australian abstains from voting. Three of the delegates vote for a federation. Seven delegates vote in favor of a two-state solution. Now they have 48 hours left to draw up two detailed proposals for the vote in the UN General Assembly. Some of them work nonstop for 24 hours.

On August 31, the 11 delegates assemble on the first floor of the UN headquarters in Geneva to present, at last, the solution to the problem of Palestine. They sign their report in alphabetical order. Over the last three months, they have received over 27,000 letters, postcards, phone calls, memoranda, and communiqués. They are tired.

Until recently, the question of Palestine and the future lay open. Now the 11 men from the neutral countries have formulated their reply and sealed it with their names.

Exactly 49 years and 364 days have passed since the Zionist congress organized by Theodor Herzl in Basel, after which he wrote: "Today I have founded the Jewish State. If I said this aloud I would be universally ridiculed. But within five years, perhaps — and definitely within fifty years — everyone will acknowledge it."

Syria

Some 300 members of the Muslim Brotherhood are undertaking military training at the agricultural training institute in al-Ladhiqia. In addition to the instruction, there are sports activities and lectures given by leaders within the movement.

Hasan al-Banna writes an article for the weekly newspaper *al-Ikhwan al-Muslimun* entitled "Let the Wind of Paradise Blow." If the Jews are preparing militarily, the Arabs must do the same.

SEPTEMBER

Stockholm

In a room looking out over a courtyard, a woman sits writing. A tiny kitchen with drying linen strung up, empty-handed, from wall to wall. A nest, a heart, a within. And as if the room were turned inside out, it encompasses everything but itself.

At night she writes, when there is calm, silence, loneliness. All that can be heard is her mother's breathing and the congested rattling of the pipes in the walls, messages from another world that will soon turn hostile. She writes the night. Or does the night write her?

To avoid disturbing her mother, no lights are lit. She lays word on word, darkness on darkness. The text forms layers over itself, as she fills the same sheet of paper with new poems, thoughts, and crossings out. Night after night, poem after poem. Nelly Sachs. No stars can be seen.

Bannwaldsee

The magazine *Der Ruf* is dead, but Hans Werner Richter and his literary friends mean to continue. They gather one weekend at Bannwaldsee, where one of them owns a holiday cottage. All 17 are asked to bring their ration cards with them. They wake at four in the morning and take the boat out onto the lake, so there is fried fish for breakfast. A luxury, and a miracle in the dilapidation of a country they call home.

Standing in stinking ruin, they seek both to convey it and to build anew. Not to look back, not to try to apportion blame — but rather to capture the shards of sky glimpsed through the bombed roof, the hope and the hopelessness among the people below, and their own belief that something different can emerge. Heinrich Böll and Günter Grass are among the future participants, those who will read their words aloud to each other, view their own writing and that of others in a mirror, find acclaim, and leave the group behind them: Gruppe 47.

Cambridge, Massachusetts

There are a thousand reasons to open a clock.

The measurement of time is subject to a mechanism. This comprises a minimum of six toothed wheels, each driving another so that each hand moves at precisely the correct speed. There is a flat spring in its case. Adjacent to it is a pinion. The pendulum swings from one tick to another. The amplitude in between is called time.

Grace Hopper is interested in calculations. She was seven years old when she opened all seven clocks at home. After that, her parents made sure she received an education in physics and mathematics. In the course of her life, she holds a string of posts that have no job title, simply because she herself invents them. Grace Hopper increasingly absorbs the future into herself.

Now she is at Harvard, having been appointed to a wartime

post as a mathematician in the US Navy — despite being a woman. (Her boss, the brilliant Mr Aiken, never tires of commenting on that fact.)

The electromechanical computer Mark II is the size of a room. The clock stands at somewhere between 15:25 and 15:45 hours on September 9 when Mark II stops working, as per usual. Grace is as familiar with the machine as she was with its predecessor, Mark I, after long shifts and meticulous logging of errors and successes. Now she finds her way into the computer in a complex ritual of error searches. She knows the pathways into the computer's inner landscape. Yet there is something incalculable, an anomaly.

In Panel F, relay #70 she finds a moth. Grace Hopper notes in the logbook: "First actual case of bug being found."

Jura

On September 11, George Orwell notes that he has to buy a wheelbarrow and that *Animal Farm* has sold out. Over the summer, he and his sister Avril have collected a total of 777 eggs.

Västerås

The idea that anyone can become anything is called the American Dream — as if everyone dreams of becoming something else, something greater and more opulent than they are, of a life in Ektachrome color film. But Europe is a black-and-white photograph. Hardly surprising then that Erling Persson makes a trip to New York to gather inspiration.

West 37th Street is home to Lerner's, a low-cost department store selling up-to-date ladies' fashion that can easily be replaced to keep pace with changing trends. Low production costs, small stocks. The idea grabs him and he makes it his own.

Back home in Västerås, Erling's father closes his own shop so he can invest in his son's project. An old fishmonger's is converted into a three-story clothes shop; fashion has as short a shelf life as a freshly caught salmon. On September 15, the local newspaper, *Vestmanlands Läns Tidning*, writes that "an attractive little shop" is opening in Stora Gatan that day. Fashion-conscious women in Västerås are now the first in Sweden to be able to update their wardrobe regularly in "the ladies' paradise" without breaking the bank. Hennes — later H&M — is a hit.

Hollywood

The time has come to investigate how much Communism Hollywood harbors. The movie industry has long been thought to attract people with left-wing sympathies, and since film itself is a powerful propaganda tool, purging anti-American elements is vital. Time to tackle the problem.

The House Un-American Activities Committee goes to Hollywood and interviews 41 "friendly witnesses." These name certain names: directors, scriptwriters, actors. The names are noted down. One of those denounced is the director Herbert Biberman, currently working on Billie Holiday's film *New Orleans*. He will prove to be a "hostile witness."

Buenos Aires

The phoenix is a recurrent metaphor in Per Engdahl's realm of thought, rebirth an obsession. Straight after the war, he renames his Fascist organization the "New Swedish Movement." New times, new labels, old dreams.

That he will collaborate on the Nazi magazine *Der Weg* almost goes without saying, especially now his old contact Johann von Leers has moved to Buenos Aires and has a strong influence on its direction. In his first article, Engdahl describes his movement from the inside:

> This group was not a party. It was an anti-Communist combat organization which openly declared its solidarity with the struggle of the German forces on the Eastern Front. That was why it was instantly branded as National Socialist by the democratic press. The baptism by fire came in May 1945. Those who had been fellow-travelers for economic reasons left without trace. Those who had been more German than the Germans themselves swiftly withdrew. But the core of the New Swedish Movement remained firm. From all directions, wise friends whispered: Keep quiet! Don't take action! Wait for the wind to turn! But we comrades looked at one another and replied: No. Someone has to hold the banner aloft. When all others flee, we remain. Only men who stand upright in the strongest headwinds deserve others' trust when the sun shines. The first public meetings were held as early as the summer of 1945 in the squares of Malmö. The local branch of the Social Democratic Party, with 40,000 members, wrote to the Swedish Government in fury: "Today, Malmö is the only

city in the world where something like this can happen." These words have never been forgotten by the comrades of the New Swedish Movement, and of all that has been written about it to date, they are perhaps the words that arouse most pride.

Per Engdahl's long article is printed in *Der Weg* No. 7, 1953. He is among friends and can express himself freely and proudly, reunited with his friend Johann von Leers, who also contributes to the same issue.

Other acquaintances and like-minded men who write for *Der Weg* in the same year include the publication's founder and permanent editor-in-chief, Eberhard Fritsch — whom Adolf Eichmann respectfully called "Kamerad Fritsch" — Hitler's star pilot Hans-Ulrich Rudel and, of course, Maurice Bardèche.

Under Johann von Leers's influence, the culture section of the magazine becomes openly Jew-hating and denialist, and it addresses itself increasingly to the Arab world. The first issue of *Der Weg* in 1953 publishes a facsimile of a reader's letter from the Grand Mufti, Amin al-Husseini, dated December 11, 1952:

> It is with great pleasure that I regularly read your publication, *Der Weg*, with its excellent articles and items ... I consider your work to be extremely important and beneficial to the traditionally friendly relations that exist between Germany and Arab society, and I hope that you will continue to have every success in the future.

Certain ideas and a certain worldview live on in *Der Weg*, and that, after all, is its purpose. In the magazine's first few years, writers who belonged to the very center of Nazi power contribute. One is Lutz von Krosigk, former Minister of Finance and Hitler's last head of government. Another is Otto Ernst Remer, the Wehrmacht officer who played a decisive part in foiling the 1944 attempt on Hitler's life, and who continued to deny Nazi genocide until the day of his death.

Then come the others: Fascist leader Oswald Mosley; Sven Hedin, a member of the Swedish Academy and a Hitler-lover; the Nazi author Hans Grimm; and Johann von Leers himself, who writes industriously under both his own name and a pseudonym. And those that take up the baton: Princess Elisabeth von Isenburg, founder and leader of Stille Hilfe, which provides financial handouts to help Nazis abscond and survive; Karl-Heinz Prieëster, one of the leaders of the Malmö Movement; and the Swedish millionaire Carl-Ernfrid Carlberg.

The editor-in-chief of *Der Weg*, Eberhard Fritsch, is not just the magazine's journalistic linchpin, he is also a key contact in the organized flow of white fugitives from Europe.

In Stockholm, the financier Carlberg has paid for the refitting of a vessel called *Falken*, which, in the spring, will take Nazis with fake passports to Argentina, under the auspices of Ludwig Lienhard. When the *Falken* leaves Sweden and is out of sight for a while, the editor of *Der Weg* asks his counterpart at the British Fascist newspaper the *Independent Nationalist* to locate the vessel. Mr. G. F. Green does as he is asked and writes about it all in a letter to a friend. Unintentionally, what is concealed becomes visible for a brief moment, like an underwater creature coming up for air before returning to the ocean's depths.

> I am asked by Fritsch to try and trace a small sailing ship, the *Falken*, which left Sweden ... with 21 Germans on board. You can guess how and why ... I am of course already in touch with Sweden, they are on the job ...

The *Falken* finally reaches Buenos Aires with its human cargo. Just a month or so later, Ludwig Lienhard describes the voyage in *Der Weg*. It is a long article illustrated with several photographs, and the whole thing sounds like a Viking voyage, a saga, an adventure.

Later, the magazine will publish portraits of the Grand Mufti and quote him on a number of occasions. After 1952, Egyptian President Gamal Abdel Nasser contributes pieces. Per Engdahl makes recurrent appearances. Oswald Mosley praises *Der Weg* as a lodestar in the darkness of Europe, a German voice from Argentina that brings encouragement and hope to its readers.

The Atlantic

The waist must be tiny, says Christian Dior. From accentuated hips, the skirt will cascade in all its lavishness, the fabric swirling as the wearer walks through the room.

The world adores his New Look, born of the tightly laced fin-de-siècle female body draped in quantities of fabric. He will be the first French couturier ever to be awarded the Neiman Marcus Award in Dallas. This means a trip to the United States.

Christian is not especially fond of traveling. It is with a heavy heart and "a thousand absolutely essential suitcases" that he embarks on the *Queen Elizabeth* in Cherbourg.

And life is not all lace flowers and champagne joy. His instant success is accompanied by French accusations that he is in cahoots with the cloth industry, that the gowns and skirts he designs which require 30, sometimes 40, yards of fabric are nothing but a trick to put the country's industry back on its feet after the war. Offended, he rebuts everything.

The journey is more agreeable than expected: far more agreeable than his reception.

Washington

With each day that passes, the lines that divide the world are more sharply drawn. The Cold War map is reduced to black and white. Power against power, light against darkness, darkness against light. Nuances of gray: nonexistent. Doubts, compromise, signs of weakness: ditto.

On September 18, the US National Security Act comes into force. One of its consequences is an intelligence agency of which many in both the US Government and the Pentagon are extremely critical — the CIA.

Dean Acheson, the future Secretary of State, warns President Truman that the new agency is structured in such a way that no one — including the president and the National Security Council — will know what is really happening or be able to control it. But his warnings go unheeded. According to the instructions issued, the remit of the new intelligence agency is to correlate, evaluate, and disseminate intelligence, and to discharge "other functions and duties related to intelligence affecting the national security."

Eleven words which will provide very useful loopholes for hundreds of covert operations.

New York

On the same day, Christian Dior disembarks in New York and is met by huge loudspeakers bellowing: "Dior! Dior!"

His relief swiftly gives way to confusion when he is led into a special room where he is exposed to flashing cameras and impertinent reactions. A press conference, this is called, though it seems more like a trial to him. His crime? Wanting to conceal American women's sacrosanct legs. Crowds of men and their wives protest against Dior's long skirts, now replacing knee-length wartime styles. And it gets worse.

In Los Angeles, he receives hundreds of anonymous letters from indignant critics who fail to appreciate what they term "the liberated bosom." In Chicago, he is met by what he calls embattled housewives, armed with criticism and placards. "Burn Monsieur Dior!" "Down with the New Look!" and "Christian Dior, go home!"

Since February, he has been accused of being immoral, showing too much, showing too little, and being both anti-feminist and misogynistic.

Christian's *femmes-fleur* with their wasp waists cause all kinds of problems. In Britain, corsets are still banned under rationing. Only those prescribed by doctors are permitted, so it is difficult for British women to dress in Dior. And with

Dior's success now universally lauded in the pages of the fashion glossies, the British Government is not amused either. Excessive domestic demand for fabric could seriously damage the weak balance of trade, it is argued, so the British edition of *Vogue* is simply banned by the Chamber of Commerce from even mentioning Dior's name.

In the streets of Paris, sensibly dressed women attack those sporting the New Look, tearing their dresses to pieces. Their anger is aroused not just by the profligacy, the profusion of fabric, which is in very short supply after the war, the multiple layers of underskirts. It is also directed at the retrograde nature of these garments, their impracticality, the tight lacing of the body they require. Coco Chanel, whose designs take quite the opposite direction, does not hesitate to criticize her rival openly: "Elegance means being free to move without restriction."

And Monsieur Dior?

Freedom has nothing to do with it, in his view; nor does the shortage of cloth. He sketches like one possessed. In his autumn and winter collection, he presents, without a second's hesitation, another creation inspired by his blithe yearning for hyperfemininity: the Diorama dress. Black wool, simple yet elegant, with a wide, sweeping, fluid skirt. Sixteen yards in diameter.

Washington

President Truman has a clear view of his future, so clear that on September 21 he summarizes the situation in his diary in a single sentence: "Have all sorts of things facing me."

True.

Szklarska Poręba

Up in the mountains, in a castle in the Polish health resort of Szklarska Poręba, 18 high-ranking leaders gather, representing the Communist parties of the Soviet Union, Yugoslavia, Hungary, Romania, Bulgaria, Czechoslovakia, Poland, France, and Italy. The autumn air is as clear as glass, the goal of the meeting an acronym.

The world has changed during the two years that have passed since the end of the war. The peaceful cooperation between the victorious powers has congealed into strategy. Europe lies between them like a game board, and each move by one party results in a countermove by the other. The Marshall Plan is no exception.

The Communist leaders who come together in the mountain village unite in their outlook: two diametrically opposed political positions divide the world. On the one side are the Soviet Union and other democratic countries, seeking to undermine imperialism and strengthen democracy. On the other side are the United States and Britain, whose aim it is to bolster imperialism and repress democracy.

It is therefore incumbent on the Communist parties to take on the special mission of protecting their countries' independence and courageously defending their democracy and liberty, without giving way to intimidation. From now on, they will cooperate with one another, share information, culture, and intelligence operations.

Two directives are issued to Europe's Communist parties from the conference at the castle in the Kamienna Valley: to combat the Marshall Plan, and to combat the Social Democratic parties that have accepted it. And these words are underpinned by others, fully audible to those to whom they apply: the message of a harder, purer, and more stringent policy in Eastern Europe. The Communist Information Bureau — the Cominform — is born.

Under Soviet leadership, the organization's purpose is clear-cut: "every Communist party is accountable to the Cominform." And: "The Cominform is the party-political foundation for the united international front. Any political deviation from that leads to treachery."

Belgrade

The Cominform's headquarters are set up in the building on the corner of Moskva Ulica and Ulica Jovana Ristića. The windows on the two lowest floors are blacked out. No fewer than 362 officials work there: 211 Russians, 17 Poles, 9 Serbs, 4 Czechs, 3 Bulgarians, and so on, reports the Swiss daily newspaper *Le Journal de Genève*. The official language is Russian. All employees are accompanied by detectives, for protection and possibly for surveillance purposes. Despite their luxurious residences and luxurious cars, the *Journal* writes, Cominform staff live like prisoners.

Cambridge, Massachusetts

Grace Hopper walks a tightrope between two languages. The field in which she establishes herself lies between machine and human.

She drinks too much, smokes too much, works too much. It is a lonely life. There comes a time when she wants to give up, but she keeps going, sobers up, and returns to the work that she herself invents.

Computers are her workmates, huge beasts to be tamed, and she becomes their tamer. Grace Hopper thinks less about what the machines actually do than about what they might do. One never knows. Just imagine. She's sure their internal workings can be modified.

This is a year when new inventions sparkle: Polaroid cameras, transistors, wireless phones. In Grace Hopper's view, it should be possible to replace all these different devices with a single one that can perform all tasks — with the right programming. But to order the machine to execute the exact request, hours of coding would be necessary. If only there were a language that could translate human commands to the machine, if only the machine could program itself, she would be spared the task.

She sits at her desk for hours on end, her head bent over her calculations. Later, when each new computer requires its own intermediary language, threatening the expanding information technology empire with fragmentation, Grace Hopper leads work on creating a single, standardized programming language, COBOL.

"I can get a computer to do exactly what I want, as long as I define it."

There are a thousand reasons to open a clock. When seven-year-old Grace Hopper opens seven clocks, there must be at least seven thousand reasons. Now she uses figures to construct a language to talk to a machine.

Buenos Aires

One of the men who arrive in Buenos Aires in 1947 is the Swedish Nazi and SS volunteer Hans-Caspar Kreuger. He works here as an instructor in the Argentinian army. He, as well, will contribute an article to *Der Weg*, but his main focus is on helping Nazis escape from Europe. For this purpose, he opens a small travel agency, which he runs together with Thorolf Hillblad, another Swedish Nazi.

Hans-Caspar Kreuger advertises in *Der Weg*. The ad states that his Skandinavisches Reisebüro advises on matters to do with immigration — "*Beratungen in Einwanderungsangelegenheiten*" — and that its offices are to be found at a familiar address, 156, Suipacha.

The same street where the Swedish Embassy is located, the same address used by *Der Weg*'s first editorial board. But there is no nameplate on the door. The Vianord travel agency is clandestine; it operates one floor further up.

A young Swede called Ragnar Hagelin takes a temporary job there in the summer of 1951. His work consists of booking passages for German clients on ships plying between northern Spain and Buenos Aires. Only German passengers. He notices that an Argentinian police inspector attends meetings every day, but draws no conclusions. What conclusions can one draw?

It is only when young Ragnar Hagelin gets embroiled in a discussion with a member of the travel agency's staff — a former athlete who competed for Hitler in the 1936 Olympics — that he realizes the context. The two men are comparing the French and German languages, and Hagelin observes that he prefers French, quotes Napoleon, and says German is for boors. At that, his colleague grabs hold of his shirt and shoves him up against the wall. Later, Hagelin discusses the incident with an acquaintance from the Swedish Embassy, who confirms his suspicions: Vianord is run by Nazis; that's common knowledge. Ragnar Hagelin hands in his notice immediately.

Do the travel agency and *Der Weg*'s editorial offices share the address simultaneously, or does one take over when the other leaves?

What we know for sure is that 156, Suipacha is a center for the flow of white fugitives from Europe.

Later in life, Ragnar Hagelin will have a daughter, Dagmar. She will be 17 years old when she "disappears," abducted by the same Argentinian military forces that were given training and instruction in 1947 by men including the two Nazis Hagelin worked for. She is never to be found again.

Stockholm

The poet Nelly Sachs has been living in Stockholm for seven years now. A refugee's life, a non-life, a life. In a poem, she writes:

> We are so sorely hurt
> we feel that we must die
> if the street throws a harsh word at us

In May 1940, Nelly Sachs, then aged 49, came to Stockholm from Berlin together with her 70-year-old mother. A late escape. Poland was already vanquished, Denmark was occupied, and in Norway the last struggles were taking place before the seizure of power became a brutal fact. The German army was on its way to France.

Why did Nelly Sachs choose Sweden? The answer was Selma Lagerlöf.

As a 15-year-old, Nelly Sachs was given a copy of the novel *Gösta Berling's Saga*, after which she dreamed and wrote in the spirit of the Nobel laureate. She even wrote to her Swedish idol and received a reply.

In Germany, Nelly and her mother were hunted down in a way that distinguishes preparation for genocide: a particular group of people are separated from the rest of the population and deprived of any means of earning a living, of their livelihoods. Soon, all that remains are the last two stages in the process: extermination itself, and the theft of all the victims' possessions.

So in November 1938, Nelly Sachs wrote to Selma Lagerlöf, now elderly and ailing:

> Can my mother and I come to Sweden, to rest with the kindest of hearts? I would give thanks with every fiber of my being for the least opportunity of life.

No reply.

A friend of the Sachs family traveled to Värmland to request Lagerlöf's help in person, but unfortunately she was hit by a bus before she could get there. Time passed. In January 1939, Nelly Sachs tried again, writing another letter. Begged, pleaded, implored, hoped.

No reply.

The injured friend wrote from hospital, and finally visited Selma Lagerlöf's estate, but the great author was taken up by building workers on the roof. Not a word got through to her. The friend waited another day and then made a final attempt, now with paper and pen at the ready to write her plea for help for Nelly Sachs in big letters. And suddenly Selma was present, ready to listen, and agreed to write a recommendation to the Swedish Government:

> It is important to me that Miss Sachs be admitted to Sweden.

A step on the way. The friend sought the assistance of Prince Eugen of Sweden, and found sponsors who could guarantee that Nelly and her mother would not be a burden on Swedish society. Sweden didn't want them, didn't want Jewish intellectuals, didn't want Jews. Only as a transit country was Sweden prepared to open up, at least momentarily and partially, and it was through that narrow crevice that Nelly and her mother slipped in.

Now they are here. A one-room flat with cooking facilities in the corner, looking out on a courtyard.

In the darkness, she writes her poems. Word upon word, ashes upon ashes, layer upon layer. Trembling, she lays poem upon poem, piling the nights into towers.

Amritsar

Sikhs armed with rifles, swords, and spears attack seven trains full of Muslim refugees. Men, women, and children: 3,000 people are murdered. The Pakistani Government now stops all trains between the Indian Punjab and the Pakistani Punjab.

Paris

A few days after Christian Dior's arrival in the United States, Simone de Beauvoir leaves the country.

She has extended her stay and spent a whole fortnight with her deeply beloved Nelson Algren. Together they have explored New York and returned to Chicago, drunk Chianti in the city's Italian neighborhood, visited the state penitentiary, listened to music, eaten rum cake, sipped whisky, and wandered through streets that seem forgotten by the world around them. Nelson talked about the Swede Gunnar Myrdal's book *An American Dilemma*, which he thinks Simone should read.

Back in Paris, she does just two things: sleep and cry. On September 27, the morning of the third day, she goes out to deal with some practical matters and runs into Albert Camus. Seeing her swollen face, he asks if she is pregnant.

Nuremberg

September 27 is also the day when the biggest murder trial of the century begins.

The 27-year-old chief prosecutor, Benjamin Ferencz, gives an introductory address opening the Nuremberg trial that will be the ninth, the trial of the *Einsatzgruppen*, and refers to the concept of genocide, even though the term still has no legal existence. I did it out of sympathy for the man, he would say later, for the kind soul in torment called Raphael Lemkin.

> It is with sorrow and with hope that we here disclose the deliberate slaughter of more than a million innocent and defenseless men, women and children ... Vengeance is not our goal, nor do we seek merely a just retribution.

Ferencz states that all law is rooted in human conscience. He calls on the court to affirm that conscience through its judgment and, through law, to strengthen fundamental human rights.

Benjamin Ferencz is proud of completing the prosecution within just two days. No witnesses are needed when the documents are so eloquent. Moreover, there is an existing testimony already on record. Otto Ohlendorf, one of the five leaders of the *Einsatzgruppen*, testified in the first major Nuremberg trial.

Is anything else necessary? Nothing else is necessary.

> Ohlendorf: In the year between June 1941 to June 1942 the *Einsatzkommandos* reported 90,000 people liquidated.
>
> Prosecutor: Does that include men, women, and children?
>
> Ohlendorf: Yes.
>
> Prosecutor: On what do you base those figures?

Ohlendorf: On reports sent by the *Einsatzkommandos* to the *Einsatzgruppen*.

Prosecutor: Were those reports submitted to you?

Ohlendorf: Yes.

Prosecutor: And you saw and read those reports, personally?

Ohlendorf: Yes.

Prosecutor: And it is on those reports that you base the figures you have given the Tribunal?

Ohlendorf: Yes.

Prosecutor: Do you know how those figures compare with the number of persons liquidated by other *Einsatz* groups?

Ohlendorf: The figures which I saw of other *Einsatzgruppen* are considerably larger.

Prosecutor: That was due to what factor?

Ohlendorf: I believe that to a large extent the figures submitted by the other *Einsatzgruppen* were exaggerated.

Prosecutor: Did you see reports of liquidations from the other *Einsatz* groups from time to time?

Ohlendorf: Yes.

Prosecutor: And those reports showed liquidations exceeding those of Group D; is that correct?

Ohlendorf: Yes.

Prosecutor: Did you personally supervise mass executions of these individuals?

Ohlendorf: I was present at two mass executions for purposes of inspection.

Prosecutor: Will you explain to the Tribunal in detail how an individual mass execution was carried out?

Ohlendorf: A local *Einsatzkommando* attempted to collect all the Jews in its area by registering them. This registration was performed by the Jews themselves.

Prosecutor: On what pretext, if any, were they rounded up?

Ohlendorf: On the pretext that they were to be resettled.

Prosecutor: Will you continue?

Ohlendorf: After the registration the Jews were collected at one place; and from there they were later transported to the place of execution, which was, as a rule, an antitank ditch or a natural excavation. The executions were carried out in a military manner, by firing squads under command.

Prosecutor: In what way were they transported to the place of execution?

Ohlendorf: They were transported to the place of execution in trucks, always only as many as could be executed immediately. In this way it was attempted to keep the span of time from the moment in which the victims knew what was about to happen to them until the time of their actual execution as short as possible.

Prosecutor: Was that your idea?

Ohlendorf: Yes.

Prosecutor: And after they were shot what was done with the bodies?

Ohlendorf: The bodies were buried in the antitank ditch or excavation.

Prosecutor: What determination, if any, was made as to whether the persons were actually dead?

Ohelendorf: The unit leaders or the firing squad commanders had orders to see to this and, if need be, finish them off themselves.

Prosecutor: And who would do that?

Ohlendorf: Either the unit leader himself or somebody designated by him.

Prosecutor: In what positions were the victims shot?

Ohlendorf: Standing or kneeling.

Prosecutor: What was done with the personal property and clothing of the persons executed?

Ohlendorf: All valuables were confiscated at the time of the registration or the rounding up and handed over to the Finance Ministry, either through the RSHA or directly. At first the clothing was given to the population, but in the winter of 1941–42 it was collected and disposed of by the NSV.

Prosecutor: All their personal property was registered at the time?

Ohlendorf: No, not all of it, only valuables were registered.

Prosecutor: What happened to the garments which the victims were wearing when they went to the place of execution?

Ohlendorf: They were obliged to take off their outer garments immediately before the execution.

Prosecutor: All of them?

Ohlendorf: The outer garments, yes.

Prosecutor: How about the rest of the garments they were wearing?

Ohlendorf: The other garments remained on the bodies.

Prosecutor: Was that true of not only your group but of the other *Einsatz* groups?

Ohlendorf: That was the order in my *Einsatzgruppe*. I don't know how it was done in other *Einsatzgruppen*.

Prosecutor: In what way did they handle it?

Ohlendorf: Some of the unit leaders did not carry out the liquidation in the military manner, but killed the victims singly by shooting them in the back of the neck.

Prosecutor: And you objected to that procedure?

Ohlendorf: I was against that procedure, yes.

Prosecutor: For what reason?

Ohlendorf: Because both for the victims and for those who carried out the executions, it was, psychologically, an immense burden to bear.

Prosecutor: Now, what was done with the property collected by the *Einsatzkommandos* from these victims?

Ohlendorf: All valuables were sent to Berlin, to the RSHA or to the Reich Ministry of Finance. The articles which could be used in the operational area were disposed of there.

Prosecutor: For example, what happened to gold and silver taken from the victims?

Ohlendorf: That was, as I have just said, turned over to Berlin, to the Reich Ministry of Finance.

Prosecutor: How do you know that?

Ohlendorf: I can remember that it was actually handled in that way from Simferopol.

Prosecutor: How about watches, for example, taken from the victims?

Ohlendorf: At the request of the Army, watches were made available to the forces at the front.

If *Einsatzgruppe* A, as stated in the report of January 1942, killed 963 people in Estonia, 35,238 in Latvia, 136,421 in Lithuania, 41,828 in Byelorussia, 3,600 in Russia —

If *Einsatzgruppe* B, as stated in the report of December 1942, killed a total of 134,298 people; and two of the units belonging to *Einsatzgruppe* C, as stated in the report of December 1941, killed 95,000 people —

If *Einsatzgruppe* D, as stated in the report of April 1942, killed 91,678; and Himmler in addition reported to Hitler in December 1942 that 363,211 people had been killed in the Ukraine, southern Russia, and Bialystok —

that totals 902,237 people.

If this figure represents two-thirds of the Jewish victims of the *Einsatzgruppen*, as the remaining third were murdered by other military units or died in ghettoes, death camps, forests, or open fields —

how many watches does that come to?

Paris

Simone suffers from waking up in the mornings without Nelson by her side. Everything feels empty. She works at Café les Deux Magots. Arthur Koestler, the writer, comes to visit her and Jean-Paul Sartre. She is sexually attracted to him, but after spending a night together she and Koestler end up arguing constantly because he doesn't consider her sufficiently anti-Communist.

Nelson has said she need only be faithful if she wants to, and she shares his attitude. But she writes sadly that she cannot share a bed with another man, she cannot bear the thought of another man's hands or lips when it is Nelson's hands and lips she yearns for so bitterly. She has turned into a conventional faithful wife, she writes, and cannot behave otherwise.

On September 30, Simone de Beauvoir finds it hard to focus on her writing. Jean Genet comes to the café and bothers her with his jokes and chitchat. She goes home to her room, with its toothpaste-pink walls, and carries on working. Deep inside, she is shaken. Never before has she let herself become as dependent on anyone as she is on Nelson Algren.

> I don't really care about anything other than you … But Canada, New York, trips, friends, I should throw everything else away to spend a longer time with you. I could have a room of my own so you could work quietly and be alone when you would wish. And I should be so nice: I'll wash the dishes and mop the floor, and go to buy eggs and rum-cake by myself; I shall not touch your hair or cheek or shoulder without being allowed to do so; I shall try not to be sad when you'll be ill-tempered because of the morning mail or for any other reason; I shall not interfere with your freedom … My own Nelson, my sweet crocodile, maybe you are smiling because you think I am so serious, maybe you think all that is just chattering like a garrulous little frog, and maybe you are right. That is why I am a little afraid of love, it makes me rather stupid.

OCTOBER

Cairo

On October 1, Hasan al-Banna sends a circular to all the Brotherhood's administrative offices, in which he urges them to make ready for jihad. He sends a telegram to the Minister for Religious Affairs, asking him to remind the imams to speak at Friday prayers about the necessity of jihad.

In another telegram to the Secretary-General of the Arab League, he states that the Muslim Brotherhood sees no way to save Palestine other than by violence. He offers the Arab League 10,000 armed men ready for combat. The Brotherhood then sets up a number of recruiting offices for the defense of Palestine, and within two days over 2,000 men volunteer in Cairo alone.

Moscow

The Soviet Union is a secret, even to itself. The bureaucracy spreads disinformation among the powerful at various levels of the hierarchy, and few know exactly what the others are up to. The outsiders who call themselves "the West" know even less. They draw the erroneous conclusion that the USSR is still a long way off having an atom bomb of its own.

Deep inside the country, the harshest times are finally giving way to change. The famine that took the lives of over a million Soviet citizens in 1946 has eased. While there may not be enough food, there is at least some. Ration cards are withdrawn. Stalin stands on the pedestal of pedestals: no one is permitted to worship anything as they worship him.

The year 1947 is a turning point. Not just because Mikhail's weapon will soon be in all combatants' hands, but also because the USSR now has the capacity to produce atom bombs. The first of these, RDS-1, is dubbed "First Lightning."

On October 10, Mikhail receives the official test results from the Soviet Army headquarters. His weapon has been selected for further development, together with two other models.

Mikhail simplifies and modifies the design. The weapon becomes lighter, has fewer components, can be subjected to rougher treatment without adverse effects. A weapon for an army of untrained men. An arm that doesn't weigh too much, that never stops working, however many blows and however much dirt and wear it is exposed to. Cheap to manufacture. Not always the most accurate of weapons, but accurate enough, and capable of being adjusted to fire single rounds or for automatic fire.

That, in the end, proves to be the decisive factor. Now the device that bears his name is selected for mass production in the USSR's armaments factories and is distributed throughout the Soviet armed forces. This weapon will adorn a country's flag, it will be used by over 50 million people in liberation struggles and terrorist acts. One day, the best-known Russian word worldwide, apart from vodka, will be Mikhail's surname — Kalashnikov.

Turin

Italian chemist Primo Levi's year seems to be shifting shape, opening up into an affirmation.

First, his serious-minded fiancée, Lucia, has been his beloved wife for a month now. Then Franco Antonicelli comes into his life, an anti-Fascist and poet in Turin who runs the small publishing house Francesco De Silva.

The publication of Primo Levi's book — the description of his year as a slave laborer for IG Farben in Monowitz, Auschwitz — is going to become a reality. Maybe the days can become lighter now; maybe his body can slough off captivity and he himself can be free, at last? He is 28 years old, and he may even be happy.

Antonicelli, his publisher, changes the title of Primo Levi's manuscript to *Se questo è un uomo* and sends it for printing. On October 11, it comes out in a print run of 2,500. Cheap paper, no advertising campaign to speak of, but at least it is there.

Turin's middle classes show some interest; the odd review is written. And that is that. Nothing more. The book vanishes. The testimony remains unheard.

Stockholm

Nelly Sachs makes her debut as a poet at the age of 56.

A poet who is both new and age-old. New because no one has ever written as Nelly Sachs writes, not even Nelly Sachs. Age-old because in her new work she transcends the here, now, then, and soon. "Living under threat," she writes, means "moldering in the open grave, without dying."

Homelessness. Neither German nor Swedish, neither Jew nor Christian, neither alone nor together: both, neither, and death flows beside everything. Nelly Sachs creates her homeland in the language of night, a place where neither history nor geography forms a boundary, and where the dead and the living walk past one another, beside one another, and exchange silences.

Someone must give a voice to that which no longer exists. Someone must give words to that which is wordless, embody that which is disembodied. In the tiny flat at the bottom of the building with squeaky pipes and hissing taps lives Nelly with her mother. Two women: the younger takes care of the older, while at the same time receiving signals from an absence and transmitting them in the form of poetry. An elegiac writer of remembrance? Memories of perceptions. Memories of extermination.

At night, the soul is not subject to the impact of the surrounding world; it is then that the stars exert their influence, and in our dreams another world appears that is otherwise invisible. At 23, Bergsundsgatan, under the meridian of the clothesline, she links herself with something that is no longer there, yet nonetheless exists. There she sits, as fragile as a memory herself, and conjures up the shades from among the dead, condensing them, making them visible as smoke.

She carries out German literature's work of mourning, someone has said. The first to create art from absence, says another. The person who proves the need to write poetry after Auschwitz, says a third.

Her German-language debut, the anthology *In den Wohnungen des Todes* is reviewed on October 13 in *Stockholms-*

Tidningen. The reviewer calls her a sister of Franz Kafka — the fourth, the spiritual sister, in addition to his three biological sisters who were murdered by the Nazis:

> Accompanied by something reminiscent of Franz Kafka's aloof smile, the anonymous suffering takes on a name and a shape. The author takes a step back, as it were, from her black-and-white images, allowing that which is human and limited to take its place among that which is unlimited and that which is beyond comprehension …

But Nelly Sachs is not a sister of Kafka. Her brothers in poetry will be quite different: Gunnar Ekelöf, 16 years younger, and Paul Celan, 29 years younger. In them she will find a sense of belonging, both wordless and rich in words. It is she, they, and lightning, breath, salt, wound. Eye, hand, throat, smoke, and ash.

Flight will be the metamorphosis that brings forth the poet Nelly Sachs. In the light of a stellar eclipse, she writes "the first letters in the wordless language." Others will soon follow, but for now it is her, and her alone.

Rogers Dry Lake

Above the desert salt flats, an aircraft breaks the sound barrier. Few pilots think it possible; human beings are not made for speeds above the velocity of sound. But pilot Chuck Yeager shows they are mistaken, and that simultaneously breaks a consciousness barrier. Other things will be possible one day. What? Everything. Supersonic aircraft, progress, conquest.

Poland

The former Prime Minister and leader of the Polish Peasant Party, Stanisław Mikołajczyk, flees the country to escape prison and a death sentence on the grounds of alleged anti-Communist activities.

Cairo

Hasan al-Banna orders his Brotherhood to make ready for jihad. On Monday, October 20, the first battalion is already on its way to battle in Palestine.

Al-Banna and the Grand Mufti carry out a joint analysis of the Palestinian problem: individual states and their governments are not to intervene in any way other than through political and diplomatic channels. Should war become necessary, it will be up to the Palestinians themselves to wage it. The people of the Arab League nod in unanimity and stand by to pay. They call in more volunteers from all over the region, train and arm them.

Kashmir

October 22. The first war between India and Pakistan breaks out.

Hollywood

Billie Holiday's director, Herbert Biberman, is questioned on October 29 by the House Un-American Activities Committee. Is he a member of the Communist Party? Is he a member of a certain trade union?

Together with nine of his colleagues, Biberman invokes his constitutional right to remain silent. The ten men wish neither to confirm nor to deny the charges. In contrast to other filmmakers under suspicion, they fight back. In the course of the public hearings, they accuse the House Committee on Un-American Activities of itself engaging in un-American activities. Every citizen has the constitutional right to belong to the political party of his or her choice, they argue jointly, and the whole basis for HUAC's activities violates civil rights.

The ten men become known as the Hollywood Ten and attract a huge amount of publicity. All are blacklisted and banned from ever again working in Hollywood. They are given custodial sentences.

Billie Holiday doubts Herbert Biberman's guilt. In her opinion, he should have screened *New Orleans* for HUAC's benefit. With all that Uncle Tom stuff the movie contains, it would have demonstrated that Biberman is a good American.

NOVEMBER

Paris

Alberto Giacometti is capable of destroying all the work he has done in the last couple of years because it isn't good enough. His friends find this very upsetting, but Simone de Beauvoir admires him for it. He has a particular conception of sculpture which he has to measure up to, so he tries time and again, never satisfied.

On November 4, Simone visits him in his studio, and while the rain falls she takes a close look at her friend. Giacometti is grubby, with plaster in his hair and on his hands, his clothes are dirty, and he looks as though he never washes. His garden is a wilderness. Next to his studio is a large, empty building, a kind of shed. The roof is full of holes. Pots and pans are placed on the ground to catch the rainwater, but they too have holes, so the water trickles out, forming rivulets and puddles.

She writes to Nelson that she has finished writing the book about her time in America and that she is reading Gunnar Myrdal's book *An American Dilemma*. The similarities between the situation of African Americans and that of women nudge Simone into resuming work on the book she has long meant to write — on the second sex. She wants it to be just as substantial and just as important a work as Myrdal's.

Jura

George Orwell types away nonstop in the upstairs bedroom, chain-writing, chain-smoking, chain-coughing. His temperature is up. The incident in August when he, his son, and two friends nearly drowned in the cold Atlantic has made his already debilitated body even more frail. He is obliged to work in bed. But he will not consult a doctor, he has no time, the book is in progress, has to be finished. He drives himself on: loose leaves, additions, crossings-out, and so the work grows into one of the most terrifying texts his publisher has ever read.

On November 7, he finishes the first draft of the book that, more than any other, defines his authorship, our contemporary world, and the fears we harbor about our future. His account of a country where the individual is always subordinate to the state — Big Brother is watching you — and where the ruling party modifies history to show that the party is always right will generate both nightmares and new words. But the book has yet to be published. He has yet to be diagnosed with tuberculosis. George Orwell is still alive. He still has a further couple of changes to make to his manuscript, and he knows nothing of the huge impact his words will have. He lies in bed after a spring, a summer, and an autumn on Jura, in the course of which he has killed adders and counted eggs, observed the shifting skies, the quantities of rain, and the breathing of the ocean. He lies in his sickbed, writing the words that will make up his last work, and names the book *1984*.

New York

Bill Gottlieb publishes his article and declares Thelonious Monk the inventor of bebop. After that, it's not long before Monk is contacted by a white married couple who come to his apartment on San Juan Hill. They sit down on the bed, their legs stretched out in front of them, while Monk takes his seat at the piano and plays with his back to them. Tune after tune. Few words are uttered, but by the time Mr. and Mrs. Lion leave, Thelonious Monk has a contract with their record label, Blue Note.

The band lineup on November 21 is George Tait on the trumpet, Sahib Shihab on the alto sax, Bob Paige on the bass, and Art Blakey on the drums. The piano isn't perfectly tuned but sounds fine. They record a total of 14 versions of four of his compositions. A single take is all they need for "'Round Midnight."

The composition has already been recorded, but never by Monk himself. That's how it is and that's how it'll stay: he writes the music, others record it. Only one other jazz composer, Duke Ellington, has more works recorded than Thelonious Monk, but then he did write around a thousand pieces. Monk wrote 70.

The fragmentary playing, the truncated snatches of melody, a kind of hesitancy that suddenly creates a breathing space — all that could be mistaken for errors or uncertainty. But it's Monk himself: it's the hesitancy, the irregular heartbeat of the times. He holds music in his hands, sculpting it.

"Sometimes I play things I never heard myself."

Never the same as other people, always his own man, unable to be anything but himself. He plays, composes, works at the piano for a week, scarcely eating, so full of musical ideas that he can't manage to write one down before it is displaced by five new ones. Then he sleeps for several days in a row.

The launch of Monk's first record under his own name creates the myth of Thelonious Monk as an oddball genius and eccentric. Success is finally within reach; no one, it seems, thinks of bipolar disorder; a myth is a myth.

Some years later, when Thelonious makes the cover of *Time* magazine, the accompanying article is entitled "The Loneliest Monk."

Husseiniyeh

Ten-year-old Meriam Othman lives with her mother, father, and younger siblings in a house in the village of Husseiniyeh, in Safad district, Palestine. Rain will fall in April, a bomb will explode in the middle of the road, a buried mine targeting the Zionists. People — she doesn't know who — will spot footprints in the mud, leading from the mine all the way to her village. The Zionist soldiers will realize that someone from Husseiniyeh is behind the bombing.

Five days of rain are followed by five days of silence. The villagers wait. The soldiers wait. Then they attack from three sides — the south, east, and west — but leave the north open. Why will Meriam remember that?

The soldiers go into the family's barn and shoot the cows. What should the family do? Meriam's father takes out a small pistol and tells his wife and children to prepare to die.

Meriam Othman, her little brother, her little sister, and the baby have to lie down on the floor. Their mother and father lay mattresses on top of them. They hear the soldiers working with spades just outside their door, digging out earth so they can reach under the house to plant a bomb. Meriam's parents lie down on the mattresses to protect the children with their bodies. Then the house explodes.

The next day, people from the neighboring village come to dig them out. Meriam is seriously injured. Her little brother is dead. Watching as they pull her sister out from under the rubble, Meriam sees that part of her skeleton is exposed. The baby lies dead, with a stone in her mouth.

New York

As though history takes abrupt turns, when it is actually slow and sluggish.

The UN Special Committee on Palestine has put forward its proposal for a partition. Now it is time for the UN General Assembly to vote. It is November 26. Everyone is gathered together in the UN building at Flushing Meadows, Queens, but as the session proceeds, the Zionists realize there will not be enough votes in favor of partition. If the vote is held today, there will be no Jewish state.

The President of the General Assembly, the Brazilian Osvaldo Aranha, advises the Zionists to play for time and drag the session out. The Uruguayan and Guatemalan delegates are prevailed upon to request speaking time, "Read from the Bible ... Read the Psalms, the promises of the Prophet Isaiah" — all to take up more time so the vote cannot be held. A filibuster.

Thus, the moment when everything is to change is delayed by 72 hours, from November 26 to November 29.

United States public opinion favors a partition. Even Americans without Jewish connections are waving placards outside the UN buildings. Influential voices are openly and forcefully advocating a Jewish state. Dorothy Thompson, one of the United States' most respected journalists and radio broadcasters, is among them. Only one other woman is more admired by the American people — year after year, the Gallup polls show the same result — and that is Eleanor Roosevelt. She, too, openly supports the Jewish state, and uses her network of contacts to influence the vote.

Under the Grand Mufti's leadership, and with strong backing from the other Arab states, the Palestinian Arabs advocate an undivided Arab state with a Jewish minority. Otherwise, their representatives reiterate, there will be a bloodbath. With 11 states already against the partition proposal, they need only to win over a further eight to block partition. There are rumors of attempted bribery and vote-buying.

And President Truman? He listens to the Palestinian Arabs' plea for the southern part of the Negev desert to remain Arab. But when that reaches the ears of Chaim Weizmann, the Zionists' leader, he travels to Washington for a meeting with Truman, who immediately changes his position. The Negev will be part of the future Jewish state.

The days and nights between November 26 and 29 are used by all parties to win votes. Serious threats are both hinted at and articulated: national threats, economic threats, diplomatic threats. The Liberian ambassador will later complain that the

United States threatened to withdraw its economic support to several countries if they voted against the proposal to partition Palestine. The Philippines were intending to vote no — it would be wrong to give someone's land to someone else — but after a call from Washington they change their decision to yes.

Haiti is promised a US loan of $5 million, so Haiti votes for a partition. Initially, France is concerned about stirring up unrest in its Arab colonies and plans to vote against the proposed partition, but has a change of heart — possibly to avoid jeopardizing Marshall Aid. Chaim Weizmann contacts an old friend, the president of the United Fruit Company, who in his turn exerts pressure on Nicaragua and other small Latin American countries. The vote is broadcast live on radio worldwide.

A majority of UN member countries now support the proposal. Thirty-three countries vote for, 13 against, and 10 abstain. The decision is taken to divide Palestine into two states: an independent Arab state and an independent Jewish one, with joint government of Jerusalem. The British troops are to pull out. By October 1, 1948, at the latest, there will be two states, with economic cooperation and protection for minorities' religious rights in place. Jubilation and pain, deep and simultaneous. November 29 is still happening.

Hasan al-Banna declares that the UN is a Russian, American, and British conspiracy under Jewish influence. The Grand Mufti urges the Arabs to join forces and annihilate the Jews the very moment that the British leave Palestine. The Supreme Muslim Council instantly calls a three-day strike. In Jerusalem, the Swedish and Polish consulates are attacked. Riots, plundering, physical violence. The Jewish terrorists of the Irgun burn down Arab property. Romema and Silwan, near Jerusalem, are attacked, as are villages in the Negev, near Kfar Yavetz, in Khisas, and in Galilee. The British troops do not intervene.

One of Palestine's most influential families, the Nashashibis, can see another solution. They are open to coexistence and a divided country, and the Zionists seek their support in the hope of an Arab uprising against the Grand Mufti that will wrest power from his hands once and for all.

But Haj Amin al-Husseini's influence is deeply anchored in family connections, wealth, the backing of the Muslim Brotherhood, and threats of violence. Moreover, many regard him as a hero, the only person who has consistently defied the British and never caved in. The Arab League supports the Husseini family, and al-Husseini himself grasps all the power within his reach. What else is the point of power?

Friendship between people, the Jewish schoolchildren who visited the school in Khirbet and were welcomed, the peace meeting between Jews and Palestinians in Samaria, the conferrals, the attempts to stave off violence before it even began — all in vain. Sandstorms, waves of wind, hopes that blow past.

In Jaffa, there is no work, but plenty of fear. Burglary and theft. The doors are flung wide open in preparation for flight, wide-open flight in a thousand directions, with a thousand nails through the heart.

In Lifta, Jewish Irgun terrorists push their way into the village coffee house and murder six men, injure seven. The children, who play while the men chat and smoke water pipes, see it all: their murdered fathers, gunned down, bleeding. After that, the people of Lifta flee too, and the stone houses on the hillsides are left as empty as the wells are unused. Until the Irgun returns and blows everything to bits.

Paris

The French postmen are on strike. No letters from Nelson Algren reach Simone de Beauvoir, and no letters from her reach him. On November 29, she sends a telegram: "Strike stops letters not my heart."

'Arab al-Zubayd

Within a few months' time, the darkness will reach the village in the mountains of Galilee; as well: dust, weapons, troops.

Sixteen-year-old Hamdeh Jom'a, her family, and all the other villagers will have to leave their homes one day in April, and go elsewhere. No place to go, just going away.

Carrying your possessions, walking. Carrying what you own, owning what you carry. Something that existed no longer exists. Weapons, loss, abandonment. The limit has reached Hamdeh Jom'a: this is the night.

All the buildings in the village of 'Arab al-Zubayd are razed, leaving the view over the valley — the river, the springs, the greenery, and the shadows — alone with itself. The cave where Hamdeh once hid, the night she stole the eggs, remains empty, echoing with gunshots. The man with the magic box will not be back; there is nothing to come back to.

Refugee camps.

DECEMBER

Stockholm

A German publisher in exile, Bermann Fischer, publishes a German author in exile. Thomas Mann's 600-page attempt to account for the moral catastrophe that overtook his native country, the novel *Dr. Faustus*, comes out.

Thomas Mann sends the composer Arnold Schoenberg a copy of the novel dedicated to "the real one."

Mann has quietly cultivated Schoenberg for years, to gather the material and the intellectual background he needs for the novel's protagonist, a syphilitic composer. He has this fictional figure invent a method of composition like Schoenberg's 12-tone technique, which he depicts as the outcome of a pact with the devil, a metaphor for the German people and their pact with Nazism.

Deeply offended, Arnold Schoenberg breaks off their acquaintance, but their quarrel becomes public. The aging composer takes exception to his life's work being attacked and politicized. Mann refers to him as "a contemporary composer" and hopes he will regard the novel as an acknowledgment of his significance to modern music. But Schoenberg takes offense at this, too. "Of course, in two to three decades, one will know which of the two was the other's contemporary."

On December 2, Schoenberg writes that art can clearly be interpreted as being Fascist, Bolshevist, left-wing, or right-wing, but music is music, art is art, and they have as little to do with freedom, equality, and fraternity as with totalitarianism.

Palestine

The first wave. Another way to describe the large numbers of people who are packing up their belongings amid gunfire and exploding bombs, under roofs where snipers lie in wait with loaded rifles.

Children and their schoolbooks, photographs, jewelry, a pipe, the infinite weight of days gone by, sensory impressions that have matured into experience. Keys on strings around their necks, on chains, keys that leave their lock, children who leave their games under rosebushes, children who leave doors and locks behind them and hang up the keys in their memories. Keys in hands, under dresses, on a chain around someone's neck, on a cord, the key cold against the skin, as unnameable as grief.

On December 4, Halissa becomes the first in a list of painful names, of abandoned olive trees and dusty roads, a list inscribed in stone, in the memories of the 750,000 people who will soon be in flight. It is followed by Haifa, Lifta, Al Mas'udiya, Mansurat al Kheit, Wadi 'Ara, Qisariya, Al Haram, Al Mirr, Khirbet al Manara, Al Madahil, Al 'Ulmaniya, 'Arab Zubeid, Al-Huseiniya, Tuleil, Kirad al Ghannama, Al 'Ubeidiya, Qumira, Kirad al Baqqara, Majdal, Ghuweir

Abu Shusha, Khirbet Nasir al Din, Tiberias, Kafr Sabt, As Samra, Samakh, Ma'dhar, Hadatha, 'Ulam, Sirin, At Tira, 'Arab as Subeih, Beit Lahm, Umm al 'Amad, Yajur, Balad ash Sheikh, Arab Ghawarina, Deir Muheisin, Beit Jiz, Beit Susin, Deir Ayub, Saris, Al Qastal, Beit Naqquba, Qaluniya, 'Ein Karim, Al Maliha, Deir Yassin, the men killed in Deir Yassin.

A few months of accumulated names: the first wave of the first wave, the beginning of a beginning. The residents who leave behind everything but their keys are the first refugees. They flee, but never cease to look back. Never.

Paris

On December 6, Simone de Beauvoir receives the first letter she has had for several weeks from Nelson Algren in Chicago. The postal strike is over at last, but what he writes worries her. He was attracted by a woman, but held back.

De Beauvoir is ambivalent. She wants him to feel free to do as he wishes, as long as he does not betray their love. Simone's trust in his feelings is such that he can go to bed with other women if he wishes. On the other hand, her physical, sexual love for him is so strong that jealousy overcomes her. But she tries to distance herself through reason from what she calls the animal instinct, which cannot be allowed to take control. Allowing him the freedom to have another woman is a gift; his abstinence is also a gift. Nothing must ever become an obligation.

Deir Yassin

Numerous isolated and vulnerable Arab villages seek non-aggression pacts with the Haganah, the Zionist paramilitary movement.

The terrorists of the Stern Gang have abducted the leaders of a village called al-Shaykh Mu'annis. The threat of violence is constant. The villagers contact the Haganah's Tel Aviv section, hoping for a reciprocal peace agreement. Haganah representatives have the abducted men released and talk to the village leaders, but no promises are made. The village, which lies on the coastal strip between Tel Aviv and Haifa, is allowed to remain where it is, the villagers to live where they live. For the time being.

Then there is Deir Yassin. A quiet village with around 700 inhabitants, a couple of miles west of Jerusalem. With the Haganah's blessing, the villagers conclude agreements on peace and good neighborliness with the two Jewish settlements of Giv'at Sha'ul and Montefiori. In return, the villagers promise not to shelter Arab insurgents.

But the agreement is a lie. The village is attacked. One hundred and thirty Zionist terrorists, defectors from the Irgun, raid the village with the Haganah's support. The terrorists are given arms, ammunition, and backup for the attack, designed to speed up the expulsion of the Arab population. It is clear that at least 110 people are murdered — men, women, and children — that corpses are thrown into wells, houses burned down, homes plundered, and villagers robbed of their belongings.

The soundwaves of the violence ripple outward. Rumors become facts and facts rumors: pregnant women slit open;

children and women raped, spat on, and stoned; men executed on the spot in their hundreds.

The Deir Yassin massacre lies a few months further on in the future, waiting to happen. The name will remain. *Al-Nakba.*

Moscow

No snow on the squares of Moscow, but good news. On December 14, those Soviet citizens who can afford to go to the cinema see a newsreel announcing their latest victory on the postwar peaceful reconstruction front: a new currency system is being introduced and rationing is being lifted. The newsreel shows beaming men and women clapping their hands. A voiceover declares that the decision fills the people's hearts with pride at their mighty Motherland and demonstrates to the world the immeasurable superiority of socialism over capitalism.

Inflation has accelerated at an ever-increasing pace after the war. Tomorrow, December 15, is the day when all the money held by individuals, cooperatives, organizations, and institutions is to be exchanged. Five old roubles will become four new ones. A victory, says the cheerful newsreel voice. The people's very last sacrifice, says the decree from the Central Committee of the Communist Party.

Up to now, Soviet citizens have been allowed a monthly ration of just 2 kg of meat, 500 g of sugar, 800 g of edible fats, 800 g of bread, and 1 kg of grain. Now rationing is over, and bread will be sold at the same price nationwide, it is promised. New prices will be set for all foodstuffs. Wheat flour and clothes will be cheaper, while the price of vodka will stay the same. Unlimited supplies of all kinds of meat will be available on the market.

On the new 100-rouble note, Lenin watches over his people.

Coburg

The publication *Der Weg* is one thing. But the European Fascists of the Malmö Movement have a platform of their own, named after the vision of British Fascist Oswald Mosley: *Nation Europa*.

It is founded by Arthur Ehrhardt, a former Waffen-SS colonel, in Coburg. The editorial board includes Per Engdahl, the Swiss Nazi Hans Oehler, and another former member of the Waffen-SS, the Dutchman Paul van Tienen.

To begin with, the main shareholder is the Swedish millionaire Carl-Ernfrid Carlberg. He will be followed by Werner Naumann, once State Secretary in Goebbels's Ministry of Propaganda, as a major financier. Later, however, Oswald Mosley will take on the main responsibility for the magazine's financial backing.

Mosley is a regular contributor to the publication and has a big influence on its orientation. The future is being built, a white bastion of visions: Europe for the Europeans.

The past is painstakingly laundered, the Waffen-SS undergoes a restoration of honor, and the genocide is persistently denied. British Intelligence describes *Nation Europa* as "having all the appearances of being the most dangerous piece of neo-Fascist propaganda put out since the war."

There are many contributors. Some of the most significant ones appear in both *Der Weg* and *Nation Europa*. Per Engdahl writes, Bardèche, Priester, Hans Grimm, Johann von Leers, Hans Oehler, Julius Evola, and Jean-Marie Le Pen.

And so it continues. If one were to take a map of the world, set these men down in their respective places of refuge, and trace lines between their names, the lines would be so numerous, so close, so all-enveloping, that the world map would become as black as a Fascist's shirt, an extinguished star.

Vienna

On December 17, Paul Antschel is issued with an ID card from the refugee holding camp in Rothschild Hospital, Vienna. The representative of the International Committee for Jews from Concentration Camps and Refugees in Vienna notes that he is 1.68 m tall, weighs 62 kg, is 27 years old, has black hair and gray eyes. His signature confirms these facts in deep-black ink.

He is one of 3,000 Romanian Jews from Bucharest fleeing from a Romanian Communist regime that seems to be turning more and more anti-Jewish, more and more menacingly unfree. The refugees leave on foot, passing through the Hungarian capital of Budapest on their way to Vienna. They sleep in derelict railway stations, bribe border guards, walk along a railway track that only a few years ago took their family members and friends to their deaths. Already there are some 200,000 refugees in Austria. Every rail sings of the present. All that gleams is due to wear.

Paul Antschel is a solitude among thousands of other solitudes, on their trudge through Europe. Many seek a home; he seeks a language.

He was born into a German-speaking family in Romania, speaks Romanian, English, French, Yiddish, and Russian, but German is the language in which he writes, thinks, creates poetry — and yet it isn't. He survived years of slave labor in the army, spent 18 months as a prisoner in a labor camp in Tabaresti. His parents, Leo and Fritzi, were deported one month before him; his father died of typhus and his mother was shot in the head. He knows their end and it is his burden. As for his poems, he writes when he can. But how can one write in a language which the murderers use? How can that language belong both to the murderers and to him — at the same time? A German bullet through his mother's head. How is he to write? His collected poems will be his way of trying to answer that question.

> You see, I am trying to tell you there is nothing in this
> world for which a poet will renounce the writing of poetry,
> even if he is a Jew and the language of his poems is German.

In Berlin, the writer Hans Werner Richter carries his conception of the new German literature like an armful of bricks, ready to rebuild the ruin. He wants the German language to be reborn, to give a voice to those who grew up under Nazism, went to war, and starved in its name, tried to survive. The aim is a new realism free of euphemism: to find "the unreal behind the real, the irrational behind reality." The new literature must begin here, and nowhere else. It must not look back. Gruppe 47 opens up for discussions, readings, and new voices.

In Vienna, the refugee Paul Antschel abides, his German poems a dance of death in words. His surname is spelled

Ancel in Romanian: now he takes it and gives himself a name that is the same but different. In the same way, he takes the German language, but rearranges the words so he can continue to dwell in it. The pain remains, but he must find different means to express it, just as he must tell of sexual desire and the absence of the dead, like a bourdon droning through the days. He must speak of all this, but in a new way, newly invented. Ancel becomes Celan, his poems emerge in a different kind of German, he is a refugee and he is a poet.

A few years later, Paul Celan will visit Gruppe 47 in Berlin, seek solidarity and dialogue, read to Hans Werner Richter and the others, but leave the gatherings with feelings hurt and heart embittered. No place for he who turns inward and looks back; no companionship offered to those seeking new words because the old words must be given a new meaning, or all the pain will have been for nothing.

How to bypass what happened? How to avoid hearing that no longer uttered? How to look ahead without catching the echo of silence? It is like killing the dead again, murdering the murdered again. Richter's ruin is not Paul Celan's.

Cairo

The clockmaker's son can admire the West for its scientific progress — but the rest? Excessive individualism has pitted man against man, and class against class, says Hasan al-Banna. The emancipation of women undermines the family. Democracy has become one with capitalism and usury, and has failed to rid itself of its inbuilt racism. Communism, on the other hand, is absurdly materialistic, and the right to speak, think, and do business exists in name only. Predictable systems, without the hidden spaces where the wonder of life blooms, without proximity to the Creator of our world. Systems in which people are too preoccupied with things, money, and the body to abandon themselves to the miraculous and to submission.

The leader of the Muslim Brotherhood declares that greed, materialism, and oppression paralyze the people of the West, undermine the social order, and destroy relationships between nations. Humanity is tormented and wretched, its leaders are following Jewish prophets, and the time has come for the East to rise.

East is East and West is West, and between them lies Palestine. The proposal for dividing the region into two states makes Hasan al-Banna decry the US as the leading imperialist state, bought with Jewish gold. Once it was the British and the French that he attacked in anti-imperialism's name, but from now on the United States becomes a target.

Next to weapons are words. Al-Banna and his successors will whet them, making them ever sharper in their struggle against the very concept of the West, as they see it.

A man who will pass on al-Banna's heritage is Sayyid Qutb, who assumes the ideological leadership of the Muslim Brotherhood after Hasan al-Banna's death.

"The cultural invasion ... makes Muslims ignorant of their religion and loads their minds with limited truths, then leaves their hearts a vacuum," writes Qutb.

He declares holy war on mental imperialism, which he considers more dangerous than the political and military varieties because it provokes no resistance. Rather, it penetrates people's minds, creating illusions of a free world. So he aims his warheads at UNESCO and other Western bodies; he aims them at "the pens and tongues" of democracy.

Sayyid Qutb is executed, considered a martyr, and attracts devoted followers. His thoughts lead on further; actions based on his thoughts lead on further. If you listen closely, you can hear devotees of violence account for murder and write the history of terror from then to now:

"The Islamic state was drafted by Sayyid Qutb, taught by Abdullah Azzam, globalized by Osama bin Laden, transferred to reality by Abu Musab al-Zarqawi, implemented by Abu Bakr al-Baghdadi."

Against the pens and tongues of democracy.

Buenos Aires

The Nazi magazine *Der Weg* is still a publication in its infancy that has not quite found its shape. But it has a dominant tone from the very first issue in 1947, and if you follow the magazine ten years into the future, you will see editor Fritsch's firm hand steering it further and further into denying Nazi genocide. Article after article marshals statistics and population figures to argue that there are actually more Jews now than before the war. The magazine also describes how specific Jews are conspiring to take over the world.

After the fall of President Perón, the atmosphere in Buenos Aires will become less Nazi-friendly. The Grand Mufti Haj al-Husseini invites his friend Johann von Leers to Egypt, where a new Nazi colony has emerged. Together, they work on the third edition of the Grand Mufti's book, *Haqa'iq An Qadiyyat Filastin.* The book is published by Karl-Heinz Priester of Wiesbaden, a close collaborator of Per Engdahl and one of the leaders of the Malmö Movement. Von Leers finds employment under President Nasser's government. According to information obtained by the Swedish Security Service, he works at the Ministry of Propaganda, organizing propaganda against Israel. Johann von Leers converts to Islam under the supervision of the Grand Mufti and takes the Arab name Omar Amin in homage to his friend.

The issue celebrating *Der Weg*'s ten-year anniversary will publish an "at home" piece on the Grand Mufti, who receives the interviewer in his "tasteful little house in the elegant Cairo suburb of Heliopolis." It will also publish a letter to the editor, printed in facsimile and signed by the Grand Mufti himself:

> The fact that *Der Weg* has been appearing for ten years now is a source of great satisfaction to me. For ten years now, you have fought tirelessly for the freedom that is the natural right, with no exceptions, of each and every nation. *Der Weg* has always supported the Arabs in their struggle for freedom and their just combat against the forces of darkness embodied by world Jewry, which have dared to rob the Palestinian Arabs of their forefathers' ancestral homeland and to steal their property. Sirs, may you continue the struggle for justice with undiminished strength, and may it be crowned with success.

New Delhi

After evening prayers at home in Birla House, people gather to receive spiritual guidance. Mahatma Gandhi again speaks of the catastrophe that is still unfolding, the agony of India, partition, and the violence against women. He often speaks of women, of those who are being abducted and raped to death. This evening, his address concerns those who have been enslaved but survived, those who have returned without noses or arms, with humiliating words carved into their foreheads and bodies. We must welcome them back, he repeats again and again on this warm evening of December 26.

> It is not a question of a mere 10 or 20 girls. The number could be in hundreds or even thousands. Nobody knows. Where are all those girls? Muslims have abducted Hindu and Sikh girls … I have received a long list of girls abducted from Patiala. Some of them come from very well-to-do Muslim families. When they are recovered it will not be difficult for them to be returned to their parents. As regards Hindu girls it is still doubtful whether they will be accepted by their families. This is very bad. If a girl has lost her parents or husband it is not her fault. And yet Hindu society does not look upon such a girl with respect anymore. The mistake is ours, not the girl's. Even if the girl has been forced into marriage by a Muslim, even if she has been violated, I would still take her back with respect. I do not want that a single Hindu or Sikh should take up the attitude that if a girl has been abducted by a Muslim she is no longer acceptable to society. We should not hate her. We should sympathize with her and take pity on her … These girls are innocent.

Paris

Simone is anxious that her handwriting is harder to read than usual on December 30. The red fountain pen Nelson gave her is broken and her writing uneven, yet she will not use any pen but this, her honeymoon gift.

> The other gift, the most precious, the silver ring, is all right. I do not put the ring away for one minute. I like this secret sign of my belonging to you.

The love between Simone de Beauvoir and Nelson Algren will last for many more journeys, letters, and visits. But Nelson will end their relationship when he realizes she will never leave Jean-Paul Sartre. They will maintain some sort of contact, although Simone will soon move in with Claude Lanzmann, 17 years her junior, and Algren will remarry his first wife. The ties will remain.

It is only when her autobiography, *The Prime of Life*, is published that Nelson Algren breaks off contact, hurt by what she has written about him. The silence between them will persist until his death in May 1981.

A few years later, on April 14, 1986, Simone de Beauvoir will be buried in the same grave as Jean-Paul Sartre in Montparnasse cemetery, Paris. On her finger will be the silver ring Nelson Algren gave her.

New York

Raphael Lemkin.

Did he know he ought to be remembered?

Did he know he would be forgotten?

He follows the *Einsatzgruppen* trial and simultaneously wages his war of writing to obtain the UN countries' support for the Genocide Convention. The beautiful world with its beautiful humanity must be protected from its own ugliness.

For Lemkin, a social and economic attack on a minority — making it impossible for them to exist — is another form of genocide. Yet the Genocide Convention the UN ultimately adopts covers physical, biological killing — but not the killing of a culture. Trying to eliminate a group of people by forcibly displacing them, creating ghettoes, or imposing forced labor is not included. Nor is banning people from using their own language, forcibly assimilating them, or destroying their cultural heritage. Too many countries want to exclude these criteria; too many have grounds too good for wanting to avoid criminalizing such actions.

Rather, the UN attaches great importance to Eleanor Roosevelt's work on human rights. In this context, human rights are assigned to each unique individual, and this — together with the Genocide Convention — will give the world's people greater protection than ever before. But in the end, this human rights document becomes a declaration, not a legally binding text.

It is easy to commit genocide, notes Raphael Lemkin, as no one wants to believe it can happen until it is too late. Out there, the world repeats "never again." But Lemkin knows the history of genocide, he knows the logic it actually follows is "next time." It has happened, so it can happen again.

The year is 1947. Lemkin has not yet read the final sentences of the Genocide Convention, which he is pushing through the

UN on his own. He has no idea that he will be nominated for the Nobel Peace Prize six times, but will never receive it. He knows nothing of his premature death, that he will drop dead at a bus stop in New York, ill with exhaustion, clasping a briefcase with a draft of his autobiography. Seven people will attend his funeral. Of all this he knows nothing.

Raphael Lemkin knows only that if the definition of the crime he has named is applied — if the murder of many can cause as much outrage as the murder of a single person — then the world will become a better place. And he signs his self-portrait in grief: "Above all that flies a beautiful soul who loves mankind and is therefore lonely."

Time is asymmetric. It flows from order to disorder and cannot be reversed. A glass that falls to the floor and shatters cannot be restored to its own completeness. Nor is it possible to identify any point that is more now than any other one.

Maybe it isn't the year I want to assemble. What I am assembling is myself. It is not time that must be held together, it is I, and the shattered grief that rises and rises. Grief over violence, shame over violence, grief over shame.

Is this my heritage, my work? Is this my principal task — to gather rain, to gather shame? Groundwater poisoned by violence.

Moving clocks run more slowly than clocks at rest. One consequence of the non-absolute nature of time is that simultaneity has no meaning. The days pass, one after the other, and I follow them. Events accumulate, one alongside the other, and I make a selection from among them. It is a simple equation, in fact: time and events, plus my selection. Result: a length of barbed wire.

It is one of the consequences of violence that people who lived before me no longer exist, that memories are annihilated, that entire universes are buried under bombed-out houses. Pain is inherited, in a steady stream from order to disorder, and cannot be reversed. There are the memories; it is in the dark that I see them, in the rain. They are my family. Darkness my light.

ACKNOWLEDGMENTS

While this book draws on a range of biographies and historical sources, the work of a number of writers has been of particular importance.

Elad Ben-Dror's research into UNSCOP, the UN Special Committee on Palestine, has been a central source. Donald Bloxham's analysis in the book *Genocide on Trial* underpins the sections on the significance of the Nuremberg trials for the writing of history. For the sections depicting Lord Mountbatten in India, I drew mainly on Stanley Wolpert's *Shameful Flight*. The section on the anti-Jewish riots in Britain is based on Tony Kushner's work *Anti-Semitism and Austerity*. The events surrounding the UN vote on Palestine are based on *A Senseless, Squalid War* by Norman Rose, while the portrayal of Thelonious Monk is drawn largely from Robin D. G. Kelley's biography of him.

I would like to thank the founders of the Nakba Archive, particularly Mahmoud Zeidan from Beirut, for their permission to make use of the testimonies they collected. Thanks are due also to Henrik Krüger, who provided information about Vagner Kristensen, Johann von Leers, and their meeting with Per Engdahl, and to Benjamin Ferencz and the late Ragnar Hagelin for allowing me to interview them.

I found further information about UNSCOP in the United Nations' Archive and Record Center in New York, such as the quotation from the Grand Mufti's diary in which he describes his encounter with Adolf Hitler.

The information about Great Britain's handling of the *Exodus* crisis and the refugee problem as a whole came from the archive of the United States Holocaust Memorial Museum in Washington.

The German National Library in Leipzig and the Berlin Center for Research on Anti-Semitism enabled me to examine all the issues of *Der Weg* from 1947 to 1956, and all the editions of *Nation Europa* published between 1952 and 1957.

I found most of the information about the people involved in the Malmö Movement in the archive of the Swedish Security Service at the Swedish National Archives in Arninge, and in the archive of the Swedish State Aliens Commission at the Swedish National Archives in Marieberg.

For information about the Ansbach camp where my father stayed in 1947, I went through UNRRA's documents in the UN Archive in New York, and received material from Yad Vashem in Jerusalem.

The year 1947 saw a number of decisive changes in the global economy — the International Monetary Fund started operations, and the General Agreement on Tariffs and Trade was drawn up — but I chose not to follow those developments.

Thanks are due to Karen Söderberg, Johar Bendjelloul, Aris Fioretos, Jonas Axelsson, Richard Herold, and, in particular, Annika Hultman Löfvendahl and Stephen Farran-Lee for discussions and for reading through the book.

Finally, I would like to thank my father for allowing me to write about him. And I would like to thank Joakim, my husband, for his patience and knowledge in our never ending discussions about 1947 over breakfast, while out walking, and at night.

Elisabeth Åsbrink
Stockholm and Copenhagen, June 2017

BIBLIOGRAPHY

Al-Uwaisi, Abd Al-Fattah Muhammad. *The Muslim Brothers and the Palestine Question 1928-1947*. London: Taurus Academic Studies, 1998.

Achcar, Gilbert. *The Arabs and the Holocaust: the Arab-Israeli war of narratives*. Trans. G. M. Goshgarian. London: Saqi, 2010.

Algren, Nelson. *A Walk on the Wild Side*. New York: Farrar, Straus, and Cudahy, 1956.

Andersson, Christoph. *Operation Norrsken: om Stasi och Sverige under kalla kriget*. Stockholm: Norstedts, 2013.

Anglo-Jewish Association. *Germany's New Nazis*. London: Jewish Chronicle Publications, 1951.

Arab Office. *The Future of Palestine*. Preface by Musa Alami. Beirut: Hermon Books, 1970.

Arnold, Anastassia. *Smertefælden*. Copenhagen: Aronsen, 2013.

Bardèche, Maurice. *Souvenirs*. Paris: Buchet/Chastel, 1993.

Barnes, Ian. "I Am a Fascist Writer: Maurice Bardèche — ideologist and defender of French Fascism," in *The European Legacy: towards new paradigms*. Cambridge: MIT Press, Vol. 7, Issue 2, 2002.

Barrett, John Q. "Raphael Lemkin and the 'Genocide' at Nuremberg, 1945–1946," in C. Safferling and E. Conze (eds.). *The Genocide Convention Sixty Years After Its Adoption*. The Hague: Asser Press, 2010.

Ben-Dror, Elad. "The Arabs' Struggle Against Partition: the international arena of summer 1947," in *Middle Eastern Studies*. Cambridge: Harvard University Press, Vol. 43, Issue 2, 2007.

———. *Ralph Bunche and the Arab–Israeli Conflict: mediation and the UN, 1947–1949*. London: Routledge, 2015.

Bergeron, Francis. *Bardèche: qui suis-je?* Grez-sur-Loing, France: Pardès, 2012.

Beyer, Kurt. *Grace Hopper and the Invention of the Information Age*. Cambridge: MIT Press, 2012.

Björk, Kaj. *Kominform*. Stockholm: Utrikespolitiska institutet, 1948.

Bloxham, Donald. *Genocide on Trial: war crimes trials and the formation of the Holocaust history and memory*. Oxford: Oxford University Press, 2001.

Boroumand, Ladam and Roya. "Terror, Islam, and Democracy," in *Journal of Democracy*. Baltimore: Johns Hopkins University Press, Vol. 13, Issue 2, 2002.

Böttiger, Helmut. *Die Gruppe 47: als die deutsche Literatur Geschichte schrieb*. Munich: Deutsche Verlags-Anstalt, 2012.

Braham, Randolph L. "The Hungarian Labor Service System, 1939–1945," in *East European Quarterly*. New York: Boulder, No. 31 of the *East European Monographs* series, 1977.

Buruma, Ian. *Year Zero: a history of 1945*. London: Atlantic Books, 2014.

Celan, Paul. *Breathturn*. Trans. Pierre Joris. Los Angeles: Sun & Moon Press, 1995. (In German, Paul Celan. *Atemwende*. Frankfurt am Main: Suhrkamp, 1967.)

Clarke, David. *How UFOs Conquered the World: the history of a modern myth*. London: Aurum Press, 2015.

Cooper, John. *Raphael Lemkin and the Struggle for the Genocide Convention*. Basingstoke: Palgrave Macmillan, 2008.

Dagens Nyheter, 1947.

Danius, Sara. "En fantastisk svensk Mann," in *Dagens Nyheter*, May 25, 2015.

de Beauvoir, Simone. *Beloved Chicago Man: letters to Nelson Algren 1947–64*. Ed. Sylvie Le Bon de Beauvoir. London: Gollancz, 1998.

———. *America Day by Day*. Trans. Carol Cosman. Berkeley: University of California Press, 1999.

———. *The Second Sex*. Trans. Constance Borde and Sheila Malovany-Chevallier. London: Jonathan Cape, 2009.

Del Boca, Angelo, and Mario Giovanna. *Fascism Today: a world survey*. Trans. R. H. Boothroyd. London: Heinemann, 1970.

Der Weg, 1947–1956.

Dewhirst, Robert, and John David Rausch Jr. *Encyclopedia of the United States Congress*. New York: Facts on File, 2006.

Dior, Christian. *Dior by Dior*. Trans. Antonia Fraser. London: V&A Publications, 2007.

Earl, Hilary. "Prosecuting Genocide Before the Genocide Convention: Raphael Lemkin and the Nuremberg Trials 1945–1949," *Journal of Genocide Research*. Basingstoke: Carfax Publishing, Vol. 15, Issue 3, 2013.

———. *The Nuremberg SS-Einsatzgruppen Trial 1945–1958: atrocity, law, and history*. Cambridge: Cambridge University Press, 2009.

Engdahl, Per. *Fribytare i folkhemmet*. Lund: Cavefors, 1979.

Feisst, Sabine. *Schoenberg's New World: the American years*. Oxford: Oxford University Press, 2011.

Fioretos, Aris. *Nelly Sachs, Flight and Metamorphosis: an illustrated biography*. Trans. Tomas Tranæus. Stanford, California: Stanford University Press, 2011.

Flanner, Janet. "Letter from Warsaw." *The New Yorker*, May 1947.

———. *Janet Flanner's World: uncollected writings 1932–1975*. Ed. Irving Drutman. New York: Harcourt Brace Jovanovich, 1979.

Frieze, Donna-Lee, ed. *Totally Unofficial: the autobiography of Raphael Lemkin*. New Haven, Connecticut: Yale University Press, 2013.

Glendon, Mary Ann. *A World Made New: Eleanor Roosevelt and the Universal Declaration of Human Rights*. New York: Random House, 2001.

Goñi, Uki. *The Real Odessa: how Perón brought the Nazi war criminals to Argentina.* London: Granta, 2002.

Halamish, Aviva. *The Exodus Affair: Holocaust survivors and the struggle for Palestine.* Trans. Ora Cummings. London: Vallentine Mitchell, 1998.

Hilberg, Raul. *The Destruction of the European Jews, Vols I–III.* New Haven, Connecticut: Yale University Press, 2003.

Hitchcock, William I. *The Bitter Road to Freedom: a new history of the liberation of Europe.* New York: Free Press, 2008.

Jakobsen, Joakim. *Tour de France: historien om världens största cykellopp*. Stockholm: Natur & Kultur, 2014.

Judt, Tony. *Postwar: a history of Europe since 1945.* New York: Penguin Press, 2005.

Kelley, Robin D. G. *Thelonious Monk: the life and times of an American original.* New York: Free Press, 2009.

Khalaf, Issa. *Politics in Palestine: Arab factionalism and social disintegration.* Albany: State University of New York Press, 1991.

Khalidi, Walid. *The Nakba 1947–1948.* Institute for Palestine Studies, 2012.

Klemperer, Victor. *The Lesser Evil: the diaries of Victor Klemperer 1945–59*. Trans. Martin Chalmers. London: Phoenix, 2004.

Krämer, Gudrun. *Hasan al-Banna*. Oxford: Oneworld Publications, 2010.

Krüger, Henrik. "Nazismen genfødtes ved Danmarks grænse," in *Politiken.* April 29, 1994.

Krüger, Henrik, and Harly Foged. *Flugtrute Nord: nazisternes hemmelige flugtnet gennem Danmark*. Lynge, Denmark: Bogan, 1985.

Küntzel, Matthias. *Jihad and Jew-Hatred: Islamism, Nazism, and the roots of 9/11*. New York: Telos Press, 2009.

Kushner, Tony. "Anti-Semitism and Austerity: the August 1947 riots in Britain," in *Racial Violence in Britain, 1840–1950.* Ed. P Panayi. Leicester: Leicester University Press, 1996.

Lagercrantz, Olof. *Den pågående skapelsen: en studie i Nelly Sachs diktning*. Stockholm: Wahlström & Widstrand, 1966.

Levi, Primo. *The Drowned and the Saved.* Trans. Raymond Rosenthal. New York: Summit Books, 1988.

———. *If This is a Man: an account of the author's arrest and deportation to Auschwitz and his experience there.* Trans. Stuart Woolf. London: Orion Press, 1959.

Lipgens, Walter, and Wilfried Loth, eds. *Documents on the History of European Integration, Vol. 3.* Berlin: de Gruyter, 1988.

Lipstadt, Deborah. *Denying the Holocaust: history of the revisionist assault on truth and memory.* New York: Free Press, 1993.

Lowe, Keith. *Savage Continent: Europe in the aftermath of World War II.* London: Penguin, 2013.

Macklin, Graham. *Very Deeply Dyed in Black: Sir Oswald Mosley and the resurrection of British Fascism after 1945.* London: IB Tauris, 1988.

Masalha, Nur-eldeen. "On Recent Hebrew and Israeli Sources for the Palestinian Exodus, 1947–49," in *Journal of Palestine Studies.* Berkeley: University of California Press, Vol. 18, No. 1, Special issue: Palestine 1948, 1988.

Mazower, Mark. *Dark Continent: Europe's twentieth century.* London: Penguin Press, 1998.

Mitchell, Richard P. *The Society of the Muslim Brothers.* Oxford: Oxford University Press, 1993.

Morris, Benny. *The Birth of the Palestinian Refugee Problem. 1947–1949.* Cambridge: Cambridge University Press, 1987.

Nation Europa, 1951–55, 1957.

Nerman, Ture. *Kommunisterna: från Komointern till Kominform.* Stockholm: Tidens förlag, 1949.

New York Times, 1947.

Olsson, Anders, ed. *Bokstäverna jag färdas i: en antologi om Nelly Sachs.* Stockholm: Themis, 2001.

Orwell, George. *A Life in Letters.* Ed. P. Davidson. London: Penguin, 2011.

———. *The Orwell Diaries.* Ed. P. Davidson. London: Penguin, 2010.

———. *Politics and the English Language.* London: Penguin, 2013.

Patterson, David, Alan L. Berger, and Sarita Cargas, eds. *Encyclopedia of Holocaust Literature.* Westport, Connecticut: Oryx Press, 2002.

Pettersson, Bo. *Handelsmännen. Så skapade Erling och Stefan Persson sitt modeförlag.* Stockholm: Ekerlids, 2001.

Pochna, Marie France. *Christian Dior: the biography.* Trans. Joanna Savill. New York / London: Overlook Duckworth, 2008.

Qutb, Sayyid. *Milestones.* New Delhi: Islamic Book Service, 2005.

Rose, Norman. *"A Senseless, Squalid War": voices from Palestine 1890s–1948.* London: Bodley Head, 2009.

Ross, Alex. *The Rest Is Noise: listening to the twentieth century.* New York: Farrar, Straus, and Giroux, 2007.

Sachs, Nelly. *Collected Poems 1944–1949* and *Collected Poems 1950–1969.* Trans. Michael Hamburger, Ruth and Matthew Mead, and Michael Roloff. Los Angeles: Green Integer, 2007 and 2011.

Sastamoinen, Armas. *Nynazismen.* Stockholm: Federativ, 1966.

Schoenberg, Arnold. "Is it fair?" (1947) in *Style and Idea: selected writings of Arnold Schoenberg.* Berkeley: University of California Press, 1975.

Schön, Bosse. *Där järnkorsen växer: ett historiskt reportage*. Stockholm: Bokförlaget DN, 2001.

Sebald, W. G. *On the Natural History of Destruction: with essays on Alfred Andersch, Jean Améry, and Peter Weiss.* Trans. Anthea Bell. London: Hamish Hamilton, 2003.

Shields, James. *The Extreme Right in France: from Pétain to Le Pen.* London: Routledge, 2007.

Spotts, Frederic. *The Shameful Peace: how French artists and intellectuals survived the Nazi occupation.* New Haven, Connecticut: Yale University Press, 2010.

Stiller, Alexa, and Kim C. Priemel, eds. *Reassessing the Nuremberg Military Tribunals: transitional justice, trial narratives, and historiography.* New York: Berghahn Books, 2012.

Strømmen, Øyvind. *Den sorte tråden: Europeisk høyreradikalisme fra 1920 til i dag.* Oslo: Cappelen Damm, 2014.

Szwed, John. *Billie Holiday: the musician and the myth*. London: William Heinemann, 2015.

Tauber, Kurt. *Beyond Eagle and Swastika: German nationalism since 1945, vols I–II.* Middletown, Connecticut: Wesleyan University Press, 1967.

Thomson, Ian. *Primo Levi.* London: Hutchinson, 2002.

Tiden, No. 4, 1956, “Nynazismen och Sverige.”

The Times, 1947.

Weiner, Tim. *Legacy of Ashes: the history of the CIA.* London: Doubleday, 2007.

Weissberg, Alex. *Historien om Joel Brand.* Stockholm: Natur & Kultur, 1958.

Wilcox, Claire, ed. *The Golden Age of Couture: Paris and London 1947–1957.* London: V&A Publications, 2007.

Williams, Kathleen Broome. *Grace Hopper: admiral of the cyber sea.* Annapolis, Maryland: Naval Institute Press, 2004.

Wolpert, Stanley. *The Shameful Flight: the last years of the British Empire in India.* New York / Oxford: Oxford University Press, 2006.

UNPUBLISHED SOURCES

Biberman, Herbert, excerpt from HUAC testimony, 1947, YouTube.

Fenyö, György, "Imperfekt om mitt liv," 2014.

Ferencz, Benjamin, interviewed by the author in May 2015.

Frischmann, Nina Ellis, and Christopher Hill, "Silence Revealed: women's experiences during the partition of India," www.academic.edu, 2010.

Hagelin, Ragnar, interviewed by the author in September 2015.

Jom'a, Hamdeh, testimony from the Nakba Archive.

Othman, Meriam, testimony from the Nakba Archive.

Rodgers, Elizabeth, and Robby Henson, *Exodus 1947*, documentary film.

Roosevelt, Eleanor, "My day," 1947, www.gwu.edu/~erpapers/myday.

Samuel, Jean, interviewed by the author in March 2004.

Truman, Harry, 1947 diary, www.trumanlibrary.org/diary.

FURTHER SOURCES

"The Austrian city Wiener Neustadt once ..."
Morgon-Tidningen newspaper, June 9, 1947.

Heinrich Himmler quotation and statistics.
Keith Lowe, *Savage Continent.*

January

"The Swedish Security Service class him as a Nazi, and after a visit to Vidkun Quisling in wartime Norway, and a subsequent journey to Finland on which he met some of the Wehrmacht's top brass, his passport has been confiscated."
Swedish Security Service file on Per Engdahl, National Swedish Archives.

On Vagner Kristensen and Johann von Leers's meeting with Per Engdahl.
Henrik Krüger, *Politiken* newspaper, April 29, 1994, and *Flugtrute Nord* by Harly Foged and Henrik Krüger.

"Even before the war he was known as the Swedish Nazi with the best connections in international Nazism."
Swedish Security Service file on Per Engdahl, Swedish State Police memorandum, September 17, 1953, H20B.

"Even now, they are setting up among themselves a well-organized system of couriers to circumvent passport, visa, and currency restrictions."
"Sverige och nynazismen," *Tiden*, No. 4, 1956.

"'Not yet hanged,' von Leers noted."
Document 018/260, Yad Vashem archive.

February

"For the sake of a senseless, squalid war with the Jews in order to give Palestine to the Arabs, or God knows who."
Winston Churchill, March 12, 1947.

On Operation Black Tulip.
Mark Mazower, *Dark Continent*, and expelledgermans.org/dutchgermans.htm.

"UNRRA's staff write anxiously to the head office in New York. They have long discussions with the kibbutz leaders ..."
UN archive S-0437.13.3.

"A UN employee summarizes the situation in a document headed *General Observations and Recommendations: the Jewish Situation in Central and Eastern Europe*."
UN archive S-0437.13.3.

March

"The sign of our times is ruins."
Hans Werner Richter, "Literatur im Interregnum," *Der Ruf*, March 15, 1947: "Das Kennzeichen unserer Zeit ist die Ruine ..."

Benjamin Ferencz and the *Einsatzgruppen* reports.
Interview with Benjamin Ferencz, May 2015.

"Creating 'serious ill-feeling between [the British and the Arab delegations to the UN] is a situation we are most anxious to avoid,' the Foreign Office notes after discussions with the Arab leaders."
FO 371/61802.

April

"They are caught between a yesterday under Hitler, when they 'never had it so good,' and a tomorrow that might turn out to be different, and might be better." Germany (Territory under Allied occupation, 1945–1955: US Zone). Office of Military Government, Education and Cultural Relations Division. German youth between yesterday and tomorrow, April 1, 1947–30, April 1948.

"The British call on France to take action to halt the flows of refugees from the French coast, in particular this American passenger vessel, the *President Warfield*."
FO 371/61805.

"... over 125,000 people are making their preparations, all of them with the same goal in mind: to reach Palestine with false papers and by unlawful means."
Information found in FO 371/61806.

Winston Churchill's speech on the "crime without a name."
Broadcast on August 24, 1941.

Raphael Lemkin's words on genocide.
Taken from John Q. Barrett's article "Raphael Lemkin and the 'Genocide' at Nuremberg, 1945–1946," 2010.

"During the war, Carlberg gathered information and advertised the publication of a two-volume 'Who's Who of Jews in Sweden,' which listed all Swedish Jews and their spouses ..."
Swedish Security Service, file P 398, CE Carlberg.

"In a complex operation, in which he was acting on behalf of both the Swedish Government and Nazi Germany in parallel, it appears that he [Ludwig Lienhard] got several thousand Swedish-speaking Estonians who were at risk of Soviet reprisals out of the country, hiding them in Stockholm with Carl-Ernfrid Carlberg's assistance."
Christoph Andersson, *Operation Norrsken*.

"The names are sent to Buenos Aires, which responds with passports and authorization to enter the country."
Christoph Andersson, *Sydsvenska Dagbladet* newspaper, January 4, 2010.

"The illegal trafficking of fugitives over the border between German and southern Jutland continues: a steady stream of white, well-educated refugees who are dispatched through Denmark to Sweden, and onward to Latin America."
Swedish Security Service, file P 398, CE Carlberg.

May

"Women are abducted, at least 75,000 women ..."
Sciences Po (Center de recherches internationales), Online Encyclopedia of Mass Violence: the Partition massacres 1946–1947 www.sciencespo.fr/ceri/en/ouvrage/oemv.

"Major Tufton Beamish: What arrangements have been made to counter Zionist plans for the illegal emigration of Jews from Europe to Palestine?"
FO 371/61806.

"Goodwill and charity are the ideals associated with the one, while national independence and a state run in accordance with Islam are the objectives of the other."
www.ikhwanweb.com/article.php?id=17065.

"After the meeting, Haj Amin al-Husseini noted down on the squared paper in his diary, in his regular, elegant hand, what his friend had said:"
Facsimile of the Grand Mufti's diary, translated in May 1947. UN archive S-0613.4.15.

"... he called on them again and again to bomb the Jews in Tel Aviv and Jerusalem."
UN archive S-0613.4.14.

"Alternatively, if every tenth American family were to take in one Jewish refugee, the problems of thousands of Jews would be solved."
Al-Uwaisi, Abd Al-Fattah Muhammad, *The Muslim Brothers and the Palestine Question.*

Andrei Gromyko's speech at the United Nations
UN archive 2/PV.77.

"Great Britain makes a request to the UN, whose Secretary-General, Trygve Lie, passes it on."
Letter of May 29, 1947, from the UN. 120.D 28a-D29. Danish Ministry of Foreign Affairs, Danish National Archives.

June

"Oh, if only we could afford to live the way we do!"
Sydney Morning Herald, June 3, 1947.

"There are days when the average German doesn't even manage the allotted daily ration of 1,550 calories."
Dagens Nyheter newspaper, February 23, 1947.

Primo Levi and Jean Samuel
Interview with Jean Samuel in March 2004.

"No compensation will be provided for damage caused by atomic bombs."
Morgon-Tidningen newspaper, June 12, 1947.

"The Foreign Office considers an anonymous campaign ..."
FO 371/61811.

"An exemplary action, and proof of their absolute loyalty to friends ..."
FO 371/61811.

"Gösta Engzell, a director-general and head of legal affairs at the Swedish Ministry of Foreign Affairs, says 'he rather fears' that many Jews in the British zone of Germany are waiting for the first opportunity to travel to Sweden."
Letter from the British legation of June 30, 1947. FO 371/81614.

"The editorial office is at 156, Suipacha ..."
Der Weg, No. 1, June 1947.

July

Letter from Ralph Bunche, July 17, 1947.
UN archive S-0605.4.5.

"Poems are written, songs intoned about liberation from the fear of death and burial under 'an umbrageous shade.'"
Al-Uwaisi, Abd Al-Fattah Muhammad cites the lyrics of such a song in *The Muslim Brothers and the Palestine Question*: "Bury us under an umbrageous shade ... we are contented to die as martyrs ..."

UNSCOP interview with John Stanley Grauel.
UN archive S-0605.4.6, conversation held on July 28, 1947.

Quotation from the former Prime Minister of France, Léon Blum.
FO 371/61820.

"Send them to the camps on Cyprus, where other Jews are gathering to wait for a visa to Palestine, or at least send them to North Africa, people write."
FO 371/61816.

"'Jews are in dangerous mood' British envoys telegraph to the Foreign Office."
FO 371/61819.

"The Jews, I find are very, very selfish ..."
Harry Truman, July 21, 1947.

August

"Synagogues in Plymouth and London are daubed with graffiti, six of the windows of the Catford Hill synagogue in southeast London are smashed by people throwing stones, and the wooden synagogue in Liverpool is burned to the ground."
Morgon-Tidning newspaper, August 3, 1947.

UNSCOP investigation among refugees.
See UNSCOP's report to the UN General Assembly, A/364, September 3, 1947, Appendix II; UN archive.

"On a block of lined paper, again and again, Raphael Lemkin scribbles the words *Quo Vadis* ..."
Raphael Lemkin papers, the New York Public Library.

"In October 1950, leading Nazis and Fascists from Italy, Great Britain, Spain, Portugal, France, Switzerland, Austria, Germany, the Netherlands, Belgium, and Sweden will meet for a conference."
Swedish Security Service, file P5134 on the European Social Movement.

"In response, he receives a letter wishing him every success, written on paper with the official Pentagon letterhead."
Archive on Per Engdahl and the New Swedish Movement: letters from Per Engdahl, dated January 16, 1951, and November 5, 1951, concerning Edward T Dickinson, Director in the Program Coordination Division, Economic Cooperation Administration, Office of the Secretary of Defense, the Pentagon.

"The word 'democracy' is left out."
Swedish Security Service, file P5134 on the European Social Movement.

"In their visa applications, the German guests give private reasons for their trip to Malmö."
Swedish Aliens Commission (Statens Utlänningskommission, SUK), secret archive, vol. E 3:1.

"He and another six Germans are refused permission to enter Sweden. They include Karl-Heinz Priester and his wife."
Swedish Aliens Commission, secret archive, vol. E 3:1.

"Other Germans protest vigorously against Skorzeny's presence. Engdahl is obliged to undo everything he has done, ring the civil servant responsible at the Aliens Commission, and ask him to reject Skorzeny's visa application."
Swedish Aliens Commission, secret archive, vol. E 3:1.

"Incidentally, Prime Minister Tage Erlander is as good as his word when it comes to fast-tracking visa applications; it takes the civil servants just seven days to reject them."
Swedish Aliens Commission, secret archive, vol. E 3:1. Tage Erlander wrote in his diary on March 16, 1951: "Per Engdahl talked about his Nazi association, which isn't a Nazi association. Even though Britain is represented by Mosley. He wants the freedom to bring whoever he likes over from Germany for his Malmö conference on April 9. The answer is very probably no, I said. Individual examination [of applications]."

"By 'culture,' we mean that which is most sacred to us. Culture is a manifestation of race. It disappears if a race disappears. For that reason, our foremost objective — preserving our culture — implies preserving our race. Given that the peoples of Europe are racially related, a European culture exists. To preserve that European culture, we intend to create unity throughout the continent."
Swedish Security Service, file P5134 on the European Social Movement.

"'... recognize and even ... assert the diversity of races,' while at the same time 'being able to call itself anti-racist.'"
Maurice Bardèche, from James Shields, *The Extreme Right in France: from Pétain to Le Pen.*

Árpád Henney and the propaganda sheet *Út és Cél.*
Swedish Security Service, file P5134.

"The request is sent discreetly to the Danish Government, which turns it down. Denmark is already overloaded with 250,000 German refugees from East Prussia and other eastern German regions who have fled before the Red Army."
Minutes of the meeting of Nordic Ministers of Foreign Affairs of August 28, 1947. 120. D28a-D29 Danish Ministry of Foreign Affairs, Danish National Archives, and Aviva Halamish, *The Exodus Affair: Holocaust survivors and the struggle for Palestine.*

"Over the last three months, they have received over 27,000 letters, postcards, phone calls, memoranda, and communiqués."
Information from an UNSCOP press release dated August 31, 1947.

September

Ludwig Lienhard on the *Falken*
"Mit dem 'Falken' auf Wikingerfahrt," *Der Weg*, No. 10, 1948.

"Per Engdahl makes recurrent appearances."
Der Weg, No. 7, 1953; *Der Weg*, No. 3, 1954.

"... other functions and duties related to intelligence affecting the national security."
National Security Act of 1947, Sec. 102 on the CIA.

"The ad states that his *Skandinavisches Reisebüro* advises on matters to do with immigration — '*Beratungen in Einwanderungsangelegenheiten*' — and that its offices are to be found at a well-known address: 156, Suipacha."
Der Weg, No. 5, 1950.

Vianord and Ragnar Hagelin.
Interview with Ragnar Hagelin on September 4, 2015.

"3,000 people are murdered. The Pakistani Government now stops all trains between the Indian Punjab and the Pakistani Punjab."
The Advertiser, September 26, 1947.

Benjamin Ferencz and the *Einsatzgruppen* trials.
Interview with Benjamin Ferencz in 2015.

Hearing of Otto Ohlendorf, International Military Tribunal.
www.avalon.law.yale.edu/imt/01-03-46.asp#ohlendorf.

Statistics on the numbers of people killed by the *Einsatzgruppen*.
Hilberg, *The Destruction of the European Jews*.

December

Moscow's currency reform.
The West Australian, December 16, 1947.

"The editorial board includes Per Engdahl, the Swiss Nazi Hans Oehler, and another former member of the Waffen-SS, the Dutchman Paul van Tienen."
Nation Europa, No. 9, 1951.

"... the unreal behind the real, the irrational behind reality."
Hans Werner Richter, referred to in: Aris Fioretos, *Nelly Sachs, Flight and Metamorphosis.*

"The Islamic state was drafted by Sayyid Qutb, taught by Abdullah Azzam, globalized by Osama bin Laden, transferred to reality by Abu Musab al-Zarqawi, implemented by Abu Bakr al-Baghdadi."
Hassan Hassan, an expert on the Middle East and a writer, "What is the IS?" BBC 4, 2016.

"The book is published by Karl-Heinz Priester of Wiesbaden ..."
Through the Eyes of the Mufti: the essays of Haj Amin, reviewed by Wolfgang G Schwanitz, at www.spme.org/book-reviews/book-review-through-the-eyes-of-the-mufti-the-essays-of-haj-amin.

"According to information obtained by the Swedish Security Service, he works at the Ministry of Propaganda, organizing propaganda against Israel."
Swedish Security Service, file on von Leers, PM 8/10 1956.

***Der Weg*'s tenth anniversary.**
Der Weg, No. 7/8, 1956.

Gandhi's speech of December 26, 1947.
Collected Works of Mahatma Gandhi, GandhiServe Foundation.

The past is never dead. It's not even past.

— William Faulkner

Also by **ELISABETH ÅSBRINK**

And in the Vienna Woods the Trees Remain

The Heartbreaking True Story of a Family Torn Apart by War

WINNER OF THE AUGUST PRIZE

An intricate weave of documents, substantive narrative, and emotional commentary that centers on a young Jewish refugee's friendship with the future founder of IKEA

"An important and urgent book... on a theme with links to our time."
—*Svenska Dagbladet*

Otto Ullman, a Jewish boy, was sent from Austria to Sweden right before the outbreak of World War II. Despite deep resistance to Jews in Sweden, thirteen-year-old Otto was granted permission to enter the country, where he found work as a farmhand in Småland and soon became best friends with Ingvar Kamprad, who would later found IKEA. Despite this friendship, Ingvar was actively engaged in Nazi organizations and a great supporter of the fascist Per Engdahl. Meanwhile, Otto's parents were trapped in Vienna, and the last letters he received were sent from Theresienstadt.

With thorough research, including personal files initiated by the predecessor to today's Swedish Security Service (SÄPO) and more than 500 letters, Elisabeth Åsbrink illustrates how Swedish society was infused with anti-Semitism and how families are shattered by war and asylum politics.

OTHER PRESS